THE SCOTTISH HIGHLANDS

Gospel and Culture pamphlets:

1. S. Wesley Ariarajah, *An Ongoing Discussion in the Ecumenical Movement*

2. Stan McKay and Janet Silman, *The First Nations of Canada*

3. Ion Bria, *Romania*

4. Noel Davies, *Wales*

5. James Massey, *Panjab*

6. Antonie Wessels, *Secularized Europe*

7. Israel Selvanayagam, *Tamilnadu*

8. Ambrose Moyo, *Zimbabwe*

9. John Pobee, *West Africa*

10. Lewin L. Williams, *The Caribbean*

11. Donald E. Meek, *The Scottish Highlands*

12. Allan K. Davidson, *Aotearoa New Zealand*

GOSPEL AND CULTURES PAMPHLET 11

THE SCOTTISH HIGHLANDS

The Churches and Gaelic Culture

Donald E. Meek

WCC Publications, Geneva

Cover illustration: The monastery at Iona (photo Robin Gurney)
Cover design: Edwin Hassink/WCC

ISBN 2-8254-1204-X

No. 11 in the Gospel and Cultures series

Printed in Switzerland

Table of Contents

Introduction

This booklet attempts to give an overview of the ways in which the Christian faith has been communicated, and its communication sustained, in the Highlands of Scotland in the context of the Gaelic language and culture of the region. The Scottish Highlands (inclusive of the western archipelago of the Hebrides) have maintained the Gaelic language since it was introduced from Ireland around the 5th century CE; it took root in most of Scotland, before receding northwards from the early middle ages.

The booklet will consider the attitudes of institutional churches and missionary auxiliaries to the Gaelic language and culture down through the centuries. In terms of modern enterprise, mission is often considered to be a relatively new activity. However, it is evident that while the methods or strategies have changed, mission has always been the charge of the Christian church. So it is important that due attention is paid to what some might see as the pre-history of Christian mission in the Highlands, and that different emphases in the churches' attitudes to Gaelic culture are properly recognized.

Attempts to communicate the Christian faith in the Highlands in the context of modern mission began shortly after 1700 — much earlier than in other parts of the world — and the area witnessed varying approaches to language and culture on the part of those bodies undertaking mission. We will explore some of the main phases and forms of missionary strategy and endeavour, together with their impact on the cultural institutions of the region.

We will also reflect on the ways in which the strategies of mission have strengthened or weakened the Gaelic language and culture. It is hoped that this will allow comparisons and contrasts to be made with the strategies of Christian mission in other regions of the globe.

The first half of the booklet (chapters 1-3) provides an historical account of the main phases and agencies active in Highland mission. It also describes the ways in which the agencies of mission observed and regarded Gaelic culture, particularly the Gaelic language. The vantage point is thus primarily external to the culture. The second half of the booklet (chapters 4-7) considers the attitudes of the various bodies, mainly the churches, to particular aspects of the culture once they had become indigenized. It also considers the manner in which recent writers have portrayed the church, and especially its evangelical Presbyterian components. The vantage point of this second part is within the culture, but the approach is, of necessity, more subjective and impressionistic.

* * *

Little study has been done recently on Highland church history, and this booklet is an attempt to fill part of that gap. Based on a series of talks and articles written mostly since 1985, it can be regarded as the outline of a larger book, and should be taken as a "first word", rather than a "last word", on the subject. For more detailed treatment of the various issues, the reader is directed to the bibliography. I am grateful to previous publishers for permission to re-use the material in this way. I also wish to thank Christopher Duraisingh for his invitation to write the booklet, and my wife, Rachel Meek, for her constant help and encouragement.

1. The Region

Definition

The Scottish Highlands and Islands can be defined very roughly as the northern half of Scotland, beyond the so-called "Highland line", drawn approximately from Helensburgh in the west to Stonehaven in the east, but excluding Fife and the coastal belt of the east and northeast, and also Orkney and Shetland. This enormous area, predominantly Gaelic-speaking in the middle ages, is fringed in the west by islands known as the Inner and Outer Hebrides, stretching from Islay to Lewis. The mainland has indented coastlines, while the central area is dominated by high mountains and deep valleys. The region has a variety of land types and land use. Some parts are very rugged indeed, with some of the highest mountains in the British Isles. Other parts — the inland valleys and straths — are gentle, flat and very productive. The islands offer similar patterns. Mull and Skye are renowned for their dramatic panoramas of mountains and rugged coastlines. The writer of this booklet comes from the Inner Hebridean island of Tiree which, in contrast to Mull and Skye, is low-lying and consists largely of what geologists call a "raised beach", with a splendid carpet of what Gaelic speakers call *machair*, wind-blown coastal sand, which has stabilized over the centuries and has acquired a rich covering of turf, ideal for the grazing of cattle. The Highlands and Islands offer an immense variety of geological forms.

The geography of the Highlands has always presented a major challenge to those who wished to spread the Christian message in the area. Itinerant missionaries have had to face unending hardship in the attempt to reach the Highlanders; often they have had to undertake a "bog-slog" through marshes, cross high mountains, endure storms, sail in tiny boats, and ride on horseback, in order to reach the population, tucked away in small settlements. It is only since 1700 that the Highlands have been opened up by modern communications such as purpose-built roads. The original road network dates from the two Jacobite rebellions of 1715 and

1745, conducted in an attempt to restore the Stewart line to the British throne.

The post-1700 effort to provide better communications was part of an overall strategy to "civilize" the "natives", who were perceived to be congenitally hostile to central government. These "natives" were speakers of Gaelic, who referred to the Highlands as *a' Ghàidhealtachd* ("the region of the Gaels"), a definition once applicable to most of Scotland. As this Gaelic culture-region shrank, its inhabitants came to be differentiated from those of the rest of Scotland by language and custom. Modern missionary outreach to the Highlands was initially stimulated by an unsympathetic, external view of the "natives" and their culture.

The geographical context

The challenge of "taming the natives" was increased by the need to conquer the geography of the region. This was one of the great stimuli to creative thinking with regard to missionary strategy in the Highlands. Ways had to be found of reaching the people where they lived, because the institutional churches, wedded to concepts like parishes with settled ministries, had difficulty in making a uniform impact across the districts under their care.

Missionary endeavour thus reflects a continuous tension between the institutionalizing of the faith and the fundamental command of Christ to go into all the world and preach the gospel to every person. Flexibility, rather than rigidity, was essential, but such flexibility could be provided only by employing the "go-structures" of mission rather than the "come-structures" of the institutionalized church. After fairly long periods of stable, institutional ministry, one can detect surges of missionary endeavour, both Roman Catholic and Protestant, often triggered by external concerns for the (re-) evangelization of the area. Itinerant preachers and catechists, supplementing the work of the parish clergy, were part of the Christian response to the needs of Highland missionary endeavour from pre-Reformation times, but the techniques had to be learned time and again, as different bodies came and went.

In fact, it is interesting to note how often the patterns of missionary strategy have been repeated in the Highlands. If the concept of "mission" can be extended back into the early centuries of the Christian era, because mission is integral to the progress of the Christian church, we arrive at places of key significance, not only in the history of Christianity in Scotland but also in early Scottish history as a whole. For example, Gaelic speakers can mention Iona with some degree of pride. This is the island to which the Irish monk Columba came around 563 CE. It could be argued that Columba's monastery at Iona was one of the earliest mission stations established in the Scottish Highlands. It is unlikely that Columba intended to establish a mission station, but there can be no question that he and his monks were among the very first to bring the Christian gospel to the Highlands. Adomnán's *Life of Columba* indicates that the saint and his fellow monks used methods which were to be repeated many times by their successors: they travelled over mountain and bog; they sailed through stormy seas in small coracles. These same patterns of mission can be found thirteen centuries later. The practical strategy of 19th-century itinerant missionaries of Baptist and Independent persuasion in the Highlands, for example, shows a strong resemblance to that of Columba and his followers.

Connections with Ireland were maintained long after Columba's time, through the networks of kin and culture that linked the Gaelic people of Scotland with their relatives in Ireland. In the pre-Reformation period the two regions shared the Roman Catholic faith, and as late as the early 17th century Ireland retained an interest in the re-conversion of the Highlands to Catholicism: Franciscan missionaries from Ireland came across in an attempt to implant a form of counter-Reformation. Here are distant echoes of the much older strategy of Columba and his colleagues. We also see the beginning of a rivalry between Catholic and Protestant activities which helped to fuel Highland missionary endeavour. Throughout the 18th century and into the 19th, Protestant missionary bodies were concerned to counteract the pockets of Catholicism which remained doggedly in the "popish parts" of the eastern Highlands, notably in Aberdeenshire, and also in the Hebrides, especially in the Small Isles (i.e. Rum, Eigg and Muck), the Uists and Barra.

In the post-Reformation period, and especially after 1690, missionary societies were established to assist the churches in surmounting the numerous obstacles to evangelization in Scotland. These bodies usually had a specifically Highland dimension, aimed at communicating the faith more effectively in the Highland cultural context. Although it can be said that mission is the work of the church as a whole, in practice most denominations created their own special missionary "wings" which tended to function as auxiliaries to the denominations themselves. The Highlands led the field in this respect. The special challenges of the region encouraged flexibility, and forced reflection on modern (post-1700) mission strategy very much earlier than was the case in other parts of the world. Later in this booklet we will consider the significance of the Society in Scotland for the Propagation of Christian Knowledge, established in 1709.

The cultural context

In addition to the major challenges posed by the geography of the Scottish Highlands, missionary endeavour over the centuries had to find a means of coming to terms with the distinctive nature of Highland culture. The Highlands were once a wholly Gaelic-speaking area. Gaelic is a Celtic language, most closely related to Irish and Manx, and more distantly to Welsh and Cornish, and it is still spoken by about 65,000 people in Scotland. At present vigorous attempts are being made to extend the use of the language, and to maintain it into the next century. Particularly noteworthy is the movement within primary and secondary education to use Gaelic as the medium of instruction for schoolchildren and thus to redress the pro-English bias which has been a feature of Highland education since the 17th century.

Gaelic was brought to Scotland from Ireland by settlers (Scotti) mainly from the Irish kingdom of Dál Riata in northeast Ulster. Migration from Ireland was underway by the end of the 5th century, with initial settlements in present-day Galloway and Argyll, and was consolidated after 500, when a second kingdom called Dál Riata was established within an area corresponding roughly to modern Argyll. The prestige of the Scottish kingdom was considerably enhanced in 563, when Columba established the monastic house in Iona. This led to a powerful alliance between the saint and the royal line, especially during the reign of Aedán mac Gabráin. The expansionist policies of Aedán and the missionary activity of Iona-based monks were influential in the first phase of the advance of the Gaelic language beyond Dál Riata. The name Atholl (from *Ath-Fhódla*, "Second Ireland") in Perthshire bears witness to early Scottic settlement beyond Argyll.

The Scotti of Dál Riata were surrounded by neighbours who spoke other Celtic languages. Chief among them were the Picts, whose principal language was essentially of P-Celtic stock (and thus related to the ancestor-language of modern Welsh). The Picts held sway over territory from the Hebrides to southern Perthshire, where they have left enduring marks in place-names (beginning with the prefix *Pit-*) and in symbol-stones, often beautifully sculptured. The Picts appear to have been absorbed gradually during the expansion of the Scots of Dál Riata, and their culture was assimilated to that of their overlords. By 847 the Picts and the Scots were under a single king.

To the south lay the kingdom of Strathclyde, whose inhabitants also spoke a P-Celtic language related to Pictish and to Welsh. Gaelic-speaking Scots appear to have been attempting to penetrate Strathclyde from the reign of Aedán mac Gabráin on, but only in the 10th and 11th centuries was that penetration sufficiently strong to overwhelm the original inhabitants and their rulers. By the early 11th century the Gaelic-speaking Scottish crown, ruling over the united kingdoms of Dál Riata, Pictland and Strathclyde, was strong enough to establish its southern boundary at Carham (1018). Only in the west was its rule in jeopardy, largely because of the presence of Norsemen, who were eventually defeated at the battle of Largs (1263). The Norsemen left their mark on the Gaelic regions, especially in areas of strong Norse settlement such as Lewis, where Gaelic dialects still retain Norse intonation patterns. In the Hebrides generally, place-names of Norse origin are very common, and some of these reflect the Christianizing of the Norse inhabitants after the year 1000, since they contain elements indicating ecclesiastical activity.

The presence of Gaelic speakers in most of present-day Scotland by 1100 is demonstrated by literary remains and place-names, many of which have ecclesiastical connections. Place-names with the element *cill*, now represented as *Kil-*, bear more general witness to the spread of the language. Some of the *Kil-* place-names derive their first element from a locative form of a Gaelic word *ceall*, meaning "monastic cell" (derived from the Latin *cella*). This is commonly followed by the name of a Gaelic saint, such as *Moire* (otherwise *Muire*) meaning "Mary" (e.g. Kilmory, Kilmuir, from *Cille Mhoire/Mhuire*, "Cell or Church of Mary"). Surviving *cill* place-names of this kind are concentrated in the west (from Kintyre to Skye and the Uists), but they extend up the Great Glen, and are present in Fife and Galloway. They may date chiefly from the 8th century. They consist mainly of dedications to specific saints, and can be construed as a reflection of "missionary endeavour" only in the widest sense. They do not imply that the particular saint visited the area, but they do indicate an ecclesiastical presence in these districts.

In the earlier middle ages, Gaelic was spoken in most of present-day Scotland, excluding (chiefly) the Orkney and Shetland Isles. "Mission" in anything approaching the modern definition dates only to the period after 1600. By that stage Gaelic was restricted mainly to the Highlands and Islands, and a language related to English, namely Scots, was spoken in most of the Lowlands and in the frontier areas of the Highlands. A north-south cultural divide gradually came into existence, signalled by the differentiation of vernacular languages.

Gaelic had begun its regression from what we now call the Lowlands by 1200. The language was probably weakest and most transient in Lothian; its gradual decay elsewhere in the south was hastened, even in areas of relative strength, by several factors, including English influences on the Scottish crown, the coming of Norman French settlers, and the establishing of burghs (towns with special privileges for trading). By 1500 Gaelic would have been spoken mainly in areas to the north of the "Highland Line", but also in Kyle and Carrick (in modern Ayrshire), and in Galloway.

"Wild Scots"

As Gaelic receded from the south, the Scottish Highlands and Islands came to be set apart from the rest of Scotland, largely by language. With a different language went a different culture and manner of life. The people who lived in the Lowlands and the eastern coastal fringe in the later middle ages, and especially the ruling bodies, came to regard those in the north as the "Wild Scots", that is, the Scots who lived in the wild, untamed, rural areas; the others were the "householding Scots". The embryo of this distinction is evident in the writing of John of Fordoun (in Aberdeenshire) in the 1380s, when he stated that "the highlanders and people of the islands are a savage and untamed nation, rude and independent, given to rapine". The fullest account of the "great divide" was given in 1521 by an eminent Scottish historian called John Mair (or Major), who wrote a famous work called *A History of Greater Britain*. He wrote:

One-half of Scotland speaks Irish [i.e. Gaelic], and all these as well as the Islanders we reckon to belong to the Wild Scots. In dress, in the manner of their outward life, and in good morals, for example, these come behind the householding Scots — yet they are not less, but rather much more, prompt to fight; and this both because, born as they are in the mountains, and dwellers in forests, their very nature is more combative.

In this awareness of cultural differentiation lay the seeds of the approach to the Highlands that became commonplace in the course of the next two centuries. The wildness of the land was matched in the pugnacious temperament of the "Wild Scots". Consequently, they were to be subdued, where necessary by weapons or, more subtly, through the attrition of their language and culture by processes which sought to integrate them into the civilized world of "Greater Britain".

Although an awareness of the "rude barbarians" of the Highlands was to contribute significantly to Protestant missionary enterprise after 1690, pre-Reformation churchmen who sought to influence the development of the Highlands and Islands were apparently no more flattering in their view of the inhabitants of the region. Thus the Foundation Bull of King's College, Aberdeen, obtained from Pope Alexander VI in 1494-95 by Bishop William Elphinstone, recognized the need to provide "the pearl of knowledge" with a view to reaching

...men who are rude, ignorant of letters and almost barbarous, and who, on account of the over great distance from the places in which universities flourish and the dangerous passages to such places, cannot have leisure for the study of letters, nay, are so ignorant of these letters that suitable men cannot be found not only for preaching the word of God to the people, but even for administering the sacraments of the church...

Admittedly, Elphinstone's "bid" may have been suitably exaggerated to impress the needs of the region on the mind of Rome, but there is much evidence that Highlanders were perceived by Lowlanders, as an uncouth people. Careerist clerics who had the care of Gaelic-speaking areas of Scotland were often Lowlanders, and they were less than comfortably at home in their adopted, or enforced, cultural context. Bishops' palaces were normally situated in cathedral cities on the edge of their extensive dioceses. In 1557 Robert Stewart, Bishop of Caithness, described his palace in Dornoch as "situated among the wild and uncivilized Scots and in a wintry region".

The gradual displacement of Gaelic from a position of importance within Scottish life reflected political and cultural change within Lowland society and the Scottish court, but it was also aided by the prejudices of both the pre- and post-Reformation churches and their leaders, who tended to accept the dominant view of those in authority in the Lowlands. This was exemplified starkly in the manner in which a group of Highland clan chiefs were compelled to give their assent to the notorious Statutes of Iona in 1609. They were invited to Iona in the autumn of 1608, on the pretext of hearing a sermon from Andrew Knox, Bishop of the Isles, "one of [King] James's most indefatigable servants in advancing the king's cause in the Isles". They soon became a "captive audience", and were bundled off to Edinburgh where they spent the winter in dungeons. Nine were then taken back to Iona, and forced to subscribe to the Statutes which, among other things, compelled them to send their eldest sons to the Lowlands for education and struck hard against several aspects of traditional Gaelic culture, including the role of the poets. The chiefs also promised to obey ministers planted in the Isles, ensure the payment of their stipends, undertake the repair of churches, observe the sabbath, and exercise discipline. Increasingly, the church, in both its Roman Catholic and Protestant forms, tended to be motivated by the practical necessity to use Gaelic, rather than by any natural affinity towards the language and the accompanying culture.

2. Mission and Cultural Context before 1750

The medieval church

Gaelic left its mark on the medieval Scottish church, and the church left its own mark on Gaelic culture. In the medieval period Gaelic, as far as we can now observe, was associated with some of the most significant parts of the normal "business activities" of the church and its patrons, though its "liturgical business" would have been conducted primarily in Latin.

Gaelic would have been used in the day-to-day conversation of the monks of the so-called "Celtic church" (or better, the "Gaelic church") of Columba and his followers. It was also employed in the composition of early hymns and in the recording of land grants, such as those noted in the early 12th century in the margins of the Book of Deer, a gospel-book associated with the monastery of Old Deer in Aberdeenshire. Nevertheless, there is a scarcity of Gaelic writing from early Scottish scriptoria. Most writing would have been in Latin, since ecclesiastical documents would have had priority, both in their creation and in their preservation. This observation holds good for the pre-Reformation church of the early middle ages, but during the period 1200-1600 we find clear evidence that Gaelic-speaking churchmen were active in the recording of sacred and secular material. The most valuable Scottish collection of Gaelic (including Irish and Scottish) poetry to have survived from the middle ages is a manuscript called the Book of the Dean of Lismore, compiled in the Fortingall district of Perthshire between 1512 and 1542 by James MacGregor, titular Dean of Lismore, and his brother, Duncan.

The MacGregor brothers wrote their material in a spelling-system based on Middle Scots and not on the "normal" Gaelic system developed by the bardic schools of Scotland and Ireland. There is good reason to believe that this Scots-based spelling-system was employed fairly generally on the fringes of the Highlands, and that its use was extended by men like the MacGregors, who were not only clerics but also notaries public, and who put into

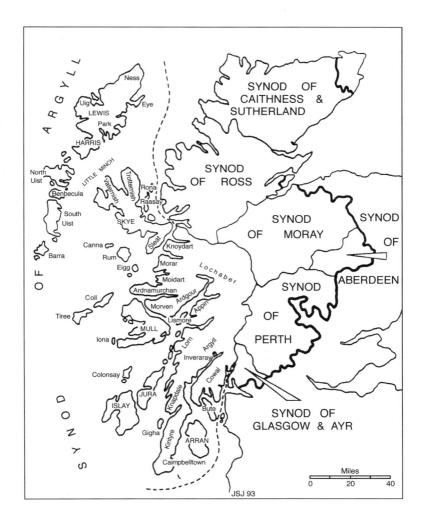

ARGYLL

Ness

Uig
LEWIS
Eye
Park
HARRIS

SYNOD OF
CAITHNESS &
SUTHERLAND

North
Uist
LITTLE MINCH
Benbecula
Waternish
Trotternish
Rona
Raasay
South
Uist
SKYE

SYNOD
OF ROSS

SYNOD
OF MORAY

SYNOD
OF

Canna
Rum
Sleat
Knoydart
Morar
Lochaber
ABERDEEN
Barra
Eigg
Moidart
Ardnamurchan
Ardgour
Coll
Morven
Appin
SYNOD
Tiree
Lismore
OF
MULL
Iona
Lorn
PERTH
Argyll
Inveraray

OF

Colonsay
Cowal

JURA
ISLAY
Knapdale
Bute
SYNOD OF
GLASGOW & AYR

Gigha
Kintyre
ARRAN

SYNOD

Caimpbelltown

Miles

0   20   40

JSJ 93

effect the form and letter of the legal system practised through Latin and Scots in the Lowlands. Churchmen of this kind, who straddled both sides of the Highland Line but had a primary allegiance to the linguistic conventions of the south, possessed the power to transform the face, if not the future, of the Gaelic language. Some came very close to doing so.

In the West Highlands and Islands (from Lewis to Islay) the Lords of the Isles held sway from about 1200 to 1493, establishing a Gaelic cultural province in the west. Within that province, the writing conventions of the Gaelic bardic schools, which trained men for the prestigious office of poet, were more rigidly preserved. The schools were responsible for the development of a classical form of Gaelic, used by the "men of letters" common to both Ireland and Gaelic Scotland, and nowadays called classical common Gaelic. The lords, who were patrons of the church, encouraged the development of a Gaelic "civil service", consisting of clerics, medical men, judges, genealogists and sculptors who were capable of writing in classical common Gaelic, the lingua franca of the literary class. Clerics and other men of letters were provided with land in return for their services. The only surviving Gaelic charter from this period, drawn up in 1408, grants lands in Kilchoman in Islay to a cleric, Brian Vicar MacKay.

The Reformation

From the very beginning of its endeavours, the Protestant church did use the Gaelic language in communicating its fundamental doctrines. Although vernacular Scottish Gaelic had begun to show features distinguishing it from vernacular Irish by at least 1300, the Protestant church adhered to classical common Gaelic as its principal medium of writing. The tradition of writing classical common Gaelic was apparently transmitted to the Reformed church through priests who had been trained in bardic schools, and who subsequently became ministers.

The most prominent of these was John Carswell (d. c.1572), the Reformed superintendent of Argyll, who translated the Book of Common Order into classical Gaelic. His work was published in 1567. As the first Gaelic printed book, it ensured that all future publications would employ the spelling system of the bardic schools (rather than the Scots-based system of the Dean of Lismore), and it set the style for future religious works. The classical Gaelic language, modified to suit vernacular Scottish Gaelic practice, is represented in the Gaelic Bible (1767-1807) and the Gaelic psalter.

The use of classical Gaelic by the Reformed church raises interesting questions, especially in light of the Reformers' strong emphasis on the vernacular language. We may suspect that the church was somewhat uneasy with the prospect of using "ordinary" Gaelic for worship in the first phase of its work in the Highlands, because the highest tradition of praise and eulogy — that of God and the secular chiefs — had been expressed in classical Gaelic throughout the middle ages. This may, in part, explain why it chose to use high-brow professional Gaelic for its foundational attempts at providing tools for the Reformed ministry.

On the other hand, John Carswell was a highly educated man, trained at St Andrews University, and also in a bardic school in either the Scottish Highlands or Ireland, where he learned to read and write classical Gaelic. We must therefore temper suspicions about any unease with the Gaelic vernacular by noting that, because of his background, classical Gaelic would have been a natural literary choice for the translator. In addition, Carswell would have seen his own peers, literate in classical Gaelic, as the readers of his book, and it would have been very important for him to have had their support for the Reformed religion. The ministers would have been expected to lead the people, and to make adjustments to the language of the texts so as to communicate effectively in their ministry. Furthermore, Carswell was well aware of the culture shared, through classical Gaelic, by the literary class in Ireland and Scotland, and he may have had his sights on Ireland too. A Protestant literary class, potentially embracing the Gaelic-speaking mandarins of both countries, would have been a major triumph for the new faith.

In employing classical Gaelic in this way, the Protestant church certainly succeeded in capturing the intellectual "high ground" of the Highlands. Members of the learned families of the classical period subsequently became ministers, and some assisted the synod of Argyll in its translation programmes in the 17th century.

Catechisms and doctrine

Several Gaelic catechisms were produced after 1630 by the synod of Argyll, and by the middle of that century it was attempting (without ultimate success) to translate the entire Bible into Gaelic. By 1659 the synod had published the first fifty of the metrical psalms in Gaelic, and it completed the task in 1694. The current Gaelic psalter derives directly from these texts, and retains a strong classical Gaelic flavour.

While acknowledging the need for a Gaelic Bible (not to be met fully until 1801), the Protestant church before 1700 put the greatest emphasis on imparting doctrinal correctness to the inhabitants of those areas of the Highlands where it was active. A concern with doctrine, and particularly with the observance of the Westminster Standards, notably the Westminster Confession of Faith (1647), has been one of the hallmarks of Highland Presbyterianism down to the present day. Indeed, the Westminster Standards have had a critical role to play in providing an overall orthodoxy which has allowed different channels of theological thought and experience to find a common focus at the formal ecclesiastical level.

The Gaelicizing of Reformed doctrine in its more scholastic form, communicated initially through translations of English Puritan and Calvinist works, was thus developed in Argyllshire, but its practical application was particularly evident in the northern Highland mainland (notably Ross-shire) by the middle of the 17th century. Ministers like Thomas Hog (1628-92) of Kiltearn became conspicuous for their powerful Calvinist preaching and their stance against episcopacy (i.e. control of the church by bishops rather than presbyters). In those parts where the Presbyterian church was active, Reformed doctrine was communicated through catechists, who examined the people in their knowledge of the shorter catechism. Catechizing in Gaelic became one of the standard practices of Highland Presbyterianism, maintaining a common core of religious knowledge.

Nevertheless, Highland Protestant theology was by no means uniform, and great care must be taken to acknowledge variations within different parts of the region. The early scholastic Calvinism of mainland Ross-shire was unknown in the island of Lewis, for example, before 1800. Within the mainland areas, different shades of theological opinion were accommodated, some of them deriving from the Lowland south, which was also the source of ongoing missionary outreach to the Highlands.

Catholicism and counter-mission

Before 1560, the Scottish Highlands, in keeping with the rest of Scotland, were Roman Catholic, although the depth of devotion would have varied from area to area. There is no single date at which the entire Highlands and Islands became Protestant; despite the vigour of the Reformed church, the transition was probably a gradual process. Traces of Catholic belief have survived even in predominantly Protestant areas until this century. The Scottish Lowlands became Protestant more rapidly and in a more tidy fashion than the Highlands, so that the cultural divide was accentuated and increased. Gaelic was equated with incivility, and "popery", as the word was, compounded the problem. Gaelic and popery were seen as the enemies of English and Protestantism, and this was especially the case when the region reverberated to the sound of artillery in the Wars of the Covenant in the mid-

17th century and the two pro-Stewart Jacobite Rebellions, in 1715 and 1745 respectively.

Of course, the perception of the Highlanders as barbarians was the view from the Lowland and non-Gaelic end of the telescope; if one were looking from the Highland end, one might have perceived things the other way round. Sometimes, indeed, the tables could be turned. After the Reformation had begun to make its mark on the Highlands, the western districts and Inner Hebrides were visited in the early 17th century by Franciscan missionaries from Ireland, and their claim — which they transmitted to Rome — was that there were so many Protestants in the Highlands that they were seriously under-staffed and in danger of their lives. The high numbers of conversions which they recorded may have reflected a desire on the part of many to escape from the yoke of "Calvinist" ministers.

The Franciscans were prepared to use Gaelic cultural conventions to gain access to potentially important converts. Thus Cornelius Ward, in trying to reach Campbell of Cawdor, took advantage of the laird's esteem for poetry, and the privileged position of poets in Gaelic society:

> Knowing, however, that Calder [*sic*] held poets in high regard, Ward, having composed a poem in praise of Calder, disguised himself as an Irish poet; then, accompanied by a singer, carrying a harp, he presented himself before Calder, and was graciously received.

Subsequently Campbell converted to Roman Catholicism.

Roman Catholic missionary activity during the remainder of the 17th century was small. A Highland mission was established in 1732, with fewer than a dozen priests by the 1760s, but reaching twenty by the 1790s. These priests were Gaelic-speaking and showed the loyalty to their traditional faith that remains a characteristic of their modern successors in the Highlands. Yet priests alone could not determine the prospects of Catholicism in the Highlands. Just as the entry of Protestantism to such areas as Argyll was helped by sympathetic landowners, so the survival of Catholicism in some of the Hebrides (notably Barra and South Uist) and pockets of the mainland (Moidart, Knoydart and Lochaber) was indebted to the support of Catholic lairds. By the end of the 18th century some of these landlords were changing their allegiance, with consequences for the religious complexion of their areas. The Highland mission itself had been weakened appreciably by the end of the 18th century, not so much by Protestant counter-attack but, as Michael Lynch points out, by "underfunding and the lack of status afforded to it throughout the 18th century, both by Rome and its better-off neighbour, the Lowland District".

Awareness of "popery" and accompanying cultural and political differentiation after 1600 directly stimulated the development of aggressive Protestant missions to the Highlands. One very influential society was established in Edinburgh with the express aim of destroying the Gaelic language and thus ridding Scotland and Britain of the menace lurking in the north. This was the Society in Scotland for the Propagation of Christian Knowledge — commonly known as the SSPCK — which was given a charter in 1709 in order to bring "civilization" (as externally defined) to the Scottish Highlands.

The SSPCK, which operated through charity schools, had a strongly anti-Gaelic policy in its initial stages, and in this respect it differed from the more positive approach of the established Protestant church, which had tried to use Gaelic constructively in the creation of manuals and catechisms for the convenience of the clergy. This anti-Gaelic route came more markedly to the fore during the latter part of the 17th century and more noticeably in the wake of the re-establishment of Presbyterianism in Scotland in 1690.

Long after the SSPCK was established, the most persistent complaint from its managers was that popery was prevalent in the Highlands, and the SSPCK's missionary programme has a good claim to be seen as a campaign against Roman Catholicism. This was one of the reasons for the SSPCK's later commitment to a vigorous publishing role. Protestant religious books were to become the counterbalance to the Roman Catholic teachings handed down by tradition and word of mouth. The provision of a Gaelic Bible was seen to be a potentially powerful antidote to popery.

The Bible in Gaelic

Given the antipathy of the SSPCK to Gaelic, it is at first sight something of a paradox that it sponsored the translation or (perhaps more correctly) the transformation of the Bible into Scottish Gaelic. By the middle of the 18th century the society had become aware of the failure of its efforts to inculcate English by disparaging and, if possible, eradicating Gaelic. In an attempt to use the mother tongue, rather than the alien English tongue, as a stepping stone to civilization, it initiated the "translation" of the New Testament into Scottish Gaelic in 1755. Eventually the New Testament was published in 1767, and the Old Testament was completed in 1801, more than two centuries after the Scottish Reformation of 1560. The men who are associated with the production of the Scottish Gaelic Bible are James Stuart (1701-89), minister of Killin, who worked on the New Testament, and his son John Stuart (1743-1821), minister of Luss, who was in charge of the work on the Old Testament.

The Highlands had not been totally devoid of Gaelic Bibles prior to 1767. A limited number of copies of both Testaments, originally translated into classical Gaelic in Ireland and published in 1602 and 1685 respectively, were brought into the Highlands at the instigation of an Episcopal clergyman, James Kirkwood. The translations had been made by clergymen within the episcopal Church of Ireland, of whom the most famous was William Bedell, an Englishman who came to Ireland as provost of Trinity College, Dublin, and died in the rebellion of 1641-2. The classical Gaelic Bibles were printed in a font based on Gaelic script, derived from insular bookhand, and as they used scribal abbreviations known within the classical tradition they were not easily accessible even to literate Gaelic clergymen of the 17th century. As a result, in 1688 Robert Kirk (?1644-92), the Episcopal clergyman at Aberfoyle, who had a fine command of classical Gaelic conventions, began the work of "converting" the classical volumes into Roman script, removing the abbreviations, and presenting the two large volumes as a single, portable pocket Bible. The new version was published in London in 1690, a remarkable achievement.

The SSPCK's Gaelic Bible (and especially its New Testament) was deeply indebted to the work of Kirk and, through him, to the classical Gaelic tradition of the earlier Irish translators. Although the language of the Scottish Gaelic Bible was (as one might expect) much closer to vernacular Scottish Gaelic in its grammatical forms and its vocabulary, it is very clear that the "translators" were using the earlier classical texts, and carried over aspects of style and idiom which belonged to the classical language. In this way, the creators of the Scottish Gaelic Bible affirmed the suitability of classical Gaelic as a major component in the language of worship in the Scottish Highlands, while simultaneously raising the status of the vernacular language.

The importance of the Scottish Gaelic Bible in stabilizing the language at a critical stage in its development cannot be overestimated. As Derick Thomson has observed, "The relatively early achievement of this canon gave Gaelic a signal advantage, for instance as compared to Lowland Scots, for it gave the language a secure and influential place in the church, and consequently in education and writing generally." The SSPCK could not have foreseen that Gaelic would have gained a "signal advantage" from their labours, but so it turned out.

From the Highlands to America

The SSPCK, established with the primary aim of bringing Christian civilization to the Scottish Highlands, became active not only in Bible translation, but also in missionary enterprise beyond the Highlands. The society supported several missionaries to the North American Indians, one of whom was the extremely influential David Brainerd. It is, in fact, no accident that the SSPCK supported Brainerd, or that it was interested in the American Indians, since the American Indians represented the same sort of "problem" as Highlanders and needed to be integrated into civilization as well as converted. In fact, the Indians and the Highlanders were so sharply focused together in the mind of the SSPCK that in 1735 they dispatched a Gaelic-speaking Highland minister called John Macleod, a native of Skye, to Georgia where he was to serve Gaelic-speaking emigrants and preach to the Indians. Lurking behind this twin-track approach to ministry was (apparently) the view that Gaelic was related to the Amerindian languages. We now know that this was not the case, but in the 18th century various misconceptions of this kind were entertained about the Celtic languages and those of other "primitive" peoples. In the mind of the SSPCK, Gaelic and Amerindian languages were comparable in another way — they were equated with barbarism and incivility, and were to be "worn out" and replaced with English as soon as possible.

It would be presumptuous to claim that the world owes David Brainerd to the Scottish Highlands, but it is very clear that mission to the Highlanders of Scotland was something of a catalyst in contributing to wider missionary endeavour.

SSPCK schools and education

School-based education, forming part of a nationwide strategy of instruction, has a long history in the Highlands. The education act of 1616 made the following provision:

> Forasmuch as the king's Majesty having a special care and regard that the true religion be advanced and established in all the parts of this kingdom, and that all his Majesty's subjects, especially the youth, be exercised and trained up in civility, godliness, knowledge and learning, that the vulgar English tongue be universally planted, and the Irish [i.e. Gaelic]

language, which is one of the chief and principal causes of the continuance of barbarity and incivility among the inhabitants of the Isles and the Highlands, may be abolished and removed... has thought it necessary that in every parish... a school shall be established...

During the 17th century parochial schools and grammar schools were established in different parts of the Highlands. Grammar schools were erected by the synod of Argyll in Inveraray in 1639, and in Dunoon in 1640.

The SSPCK thus supplemented existing schools, some of which already implemented anti-Gaelic policies, but it appears to have brought a sharper edge to the strategy for eradicating "barbarity and incivility" from the Highlands. Dedicated to the implanting of English, it saw the school as a very effective missionary agency. However, by trying to knock Gaelic directly out of the heads of its scholars, in order to replace it with English, it produced pupils who remained illiterate in both languages. After fifty years of failure, it changed its tactics, and produced fundamentally important texts in Scottish Gaelic (as indicated in the discussion of the Scottish Gaelic New Testament of 1767).

While noting the use of the school as an agency of mission, especially mission which is hostile to the indigenous culture, we should nevertheless be aware that the SSPCK was not without Gaelic-speaking workers of a very influential kind. It employed two of the premier Gaelic poets of the 18th century as schoolmasters, Alexander MacDonald (c.1695-c.1770) in Ardnamurchan, and Dugald Buchanan (1716-68), in Kinloch Rannoch, Perthshire. While in the service of the SSPCK, MacDonald produced his Gaelic-English vocabulary of 1741, before abandoning his school shortly before the arrival of Prince Charles at the beginning of the 1745 Jacobite Rebellion. MacDonald also espoused Catholicism, and became an ardent poet of the Jacobite cause. In this way, the anti-Gaelic policies of the SSPCK appear to have produced "reverse cultural thrust". Dugald Buchanan, on the other hand, became the first major evangelical poet of the Gaelic world. His poems (only eight in number) were published in 1767, the same year he was in Edinburgh supervising the printing of the Gaelic New Testament. Curiously, substantial sections of some of his poems are unacknowledged translations or paraphrases of hymns by the "father of English hymnody", Isaac Watts (1674-1748), with some further influence from the works of James Thomson and Edward Young and others of the "Graveyard School" of poets. Spiritual power from the Lowlands and England contributed very substantially to the making of "Highland religion".

The school-based missionary model used by the SSPCK was exported to other parts of the world. Alexander Duff (1806-78), one of the most famous names in Scottish missionary history and himself a Gaelic-speaking Highlander from Perthshire, was apparently influenced by SSPCK philosophy in choosing the pro-English methods of education which he employed in Calcutta.

Despite its manifest shortcomings, the SSPCK's approach was used productively in the Highlands. The society's main school, Raining's School in Inverness, trained several of the most influential Gaelic scholars and ministers who were active in the Highlands. Raining's (named after an English merchant who endowed it in the 18th century) was at the peak of academic excellence at the end of the 19th century. Its most distinguished headmaster was Alexander MacBain (1855-1907), an outstanding Gaelic scholar who can fairly be regarded as the father of modern Celtic studies in Scotland. Gaelic literature and scholarship thus owe much to the investments of the SSPCK.

3. Mission and Cultural Context after 1750

Although parts of the Highlands such as Ross-shire and Sutherland had been imbued with Puritan doctrine in the 17th century, the established church in the Highlands as a whole was not identified with evangelicalism before 1800. Post-1800 evangelicalism (which tended to place more emphasis on "affections" and emotions than did doctrinal Puritanism) was propelled by, and contributed to, a fresh surge of missionary endeavour; it spread slowly, entering the southern fringes of the Highlands, notably Perthshire, and extending gradually northwards to Skye (1806) and Lewis (by 1820).

The palpable lack of "vital Christianity" in these southern districts (to say nothing of the more isolated northern areas) was what attracted the new evangelical interest. Its preachers found ready audiences in parishes which had ministers of the non-evangelical, so-called Moderate kind, who upheld moral virtues and were not troubled by "the religion of the heart". The new wave of missionary activity, which gradually overlaid the earlier Puritanism in the northern mainland, was to have profound consequences for the general character of Presbyterianism in the Highlands, since it was directly concerned with the salvation of the Highland people, and did not regard "civilization" or culture, Gaelic or otherwise, as an essential prerequisite for the implantation of the faith. Highlanders, who were sometimes designated as "barbarians" by the new enthusiasts, were seen to be in spiritual, rather than cultural, darkness.

The evangelical revival and Methodist interest

In shifting the emphasis of missionary activity from civilization (in "English" terms) to salvation as the first priority, the evangelical revival of the mid-18th century was of great importance. The revival deeply influenced Wales and England, and it had close links with the Great Awakening in the United States. The effect of the revival on Scotland was not immediate or dramatic, but it was certainly noticeable. The visits of John Wesley and George Whitefield to

Scotland, while they were not always appreciated at the time, were a sure indication that new forces were at work. These forces were apparent in the Cambuslang revival of 1742 and subsequent revival movements which affected both the Lowlands and the Highlands, especially the border areas between them. Highlanders, such as the Gaelic hymnwriter Dugald Buchanan, travelled to the centres of revival in the south, and took the new impulses back to the Highlands.

Methodists led the new wave of missionary interest. The well-known Methodist missionary Thomas Coke visited Scotland about the end of 1785, and evidently had contact with the Gaelic-speaking areas. Describing Highlanders as "little better than the rudest barbarians", Coke designated the Highlands as the first of the mission fields for which he made his 1786 appeal, believing that Gaelic-speaking missionaries could be found who would put his plan into effect. Indeed, he had already found one such missionary: this was Duncan McAllum, a native of Argyll, who initially wished to go to Africa but to whom John Wesley gave "an unlimited commission to visit the Highlands and adjacent islands of Scotland". This roving commission was not, as far as we know, put into full effect. McAllum was assigned to the town of Ayr, and it was probably Coke's intention (and Wesley's) that he should begin by preaching to the Highlanders who had migrated to that town. It is highly likely that such migrants would have been from Argyll and the Clyde islands such as Arran and Bute. McAllum, apparently, later evangelized in Strathspey, but Coke's overall plan did not come to fruition.

In 1808 Coke revived the idea of appointing a Gaelic-speaking missionary, who was to be based in Inverness, and once more a suitable candidate, Hugh McKay, was designated for work. However, McKay's missionary status was withdrawn so that he could fill a vacancy in Inverness itself. Thereafter the Methodist interest in the Gaelic-speaking Highlands was abandoned, much to the regret of Coke, who believed that the plan had never been given a fair trial. The

Methodists' failure in the Highlands highlighted the problems of recruitment and strategy confronting would-be missionary bodies in the area.

Dissenters and Highland missions, 1797-1850

The key to the post-1790 enthusiasm for Highland missionary enterprise lies in the surge of interest in foreign
missionary activity which appeared in the 1790s in the wake
of the evangelical revival, and especially William Carey's
departure to India in 1793. This interest was especially
strong among dissenting churches and dissenting bodies in
England, although evangelicals in the Anglican church were
also involved. In Scotland too, the initiative lay with the
dissenting bodies, principally Independents (Congregationalists) and Baptists, with some support on an individual basis
from evangelicals within the established church. The Relief
Church and the United Secession Church (both Presbyterian)
were also interested in mission. All of these bodies were
active in the Highlands. The Relief Church was evidently the
first body to mount a specific mission to the region in 1797.

Some bodies were more successful than others, and
some degree of regional variation is evident. Independents
and Baptists established themselves more firmly in the
southern Highlands and Islands than in the northern parts.
Their capacity to establish themselves depended on the
accessibility of the parish church, the presence or absence
of the minister, and his theological affiliation (i.e. whether
he was a Moderate or an evangelical). The bodies which
met with the greatest success were those that had as yet no
denominational identity. The denominational churches —
the Relief and the United Secession in this case — failed to
make any major impact largely because they were not as
flexible in the matter of recruitment and training as the
Independents and Baptists, who were much more willing to
create small societies aimed directly at Highland mission
and targeted on specific parts of the Highlands. This,
however, failed to promote strength or cohesion, and

although Baptists and Independents planted churches, some of which still survive in the Inner Hebrides (e.g. Tiree, Islay, Colonsay and Mull) and on the western mainland, they failed to make a major denominational impact on the Highlands as whole. In areas where new churches took root, emigration often weakened the cause, particularly in the period from 1830 to 1850.

The effectiveness of the new missionary societies operating in the Highlands around 1800 was seriously hampered not only by social change but also by several factors pertaining to their structures. The most serious flaw was that they were too dependent on individual benefactors. Power rested with a small group of men, or might even be concentrated in the hands of a single individual. In 1797, for instance, the brothers Robert and James Haldane, who had originally intended to go to India as missionaries, set up the Society for Propagating the Gospel at Home to promote itinerant evangelism in Scotland generally, but with a specific remit for the Highlands. The Haldanes, who had become Independents by 1798, trained and funded their own preachers and established a remarkable framework for evangelistic endeavour which was entirely self-supporting. Therein lay its strength and its weakness. When the Haldanes became Baptists in 1808, their society collapsed and was not replaced by a directly comparable organization. Instead, the Haldanes promoted missionary work from their Tabernacle in Leith Walk, Edinburgh, and if anything adhered more strictly to independent principles than they had done before 1808. A society had been replaced by a single church. Among Baptists too, the initiative rested very firmly with individual leaders and occasionally with individual congregations. In 1807-8 the Edinburgh Baptist pastor Christopher Anderson, influenced initially by the example of Carey, established a society for Highland and rural mission. Anderson became the mainspring of the society, which began its work by employing a single missionary in Perthshire in 1808, and another in Argyll in 1810.

The individualistic nature of these missionary bodies curtailed their capacity to raise funds. As the original patrons' resources declined, a broader base of support had to be found. The Independents (or Congregationalists) were more willing than Baptists to cooperate with other bodies in the formation of broadly-based interdenominational missionary societies for the support of the work in the Highlands. In 1817 a missionary society was formed at Paisley, with the title "The Society in Paisley and its Vicinity for Gaelic Missions to the Highlands and Islands of Scotland". This society had a strong Congregationalist interest, but it also supported missionaries from the Relief Church and the Antiburghers. In 1820 the Highland Missionary Society was formed in Edinburgh, mainly to provide financial support for candidates from the Highlands who were being trained by the Presbyterian and Congregational churches. It gave particular assistance to members of the Relief and United Secession churches.

Doctrinal differences further restricted the cumulative impact of the societies. There were, for instance, two different types of Baptists who were active in the Highlands, and they did not see eye to eye with each other on matters of church polity. Christopher Anderson was what is termed an "English" Baptist, and he had little time for what were termed "Scotch Baptists" (the older stock, who believed in a plurality of teaching elders in a church, rather than the single pastor favoured by the "English" style). The Scotch Baptists funded the Baptist Highland Mission, a society formed in 1816 to provide resources for Baptist missionaries stationed in Perthshire.

Altogether, it was a rather untidy approach, but financial difficulties encouraged some degree of cooperation. Unification of the Baptist agencies came in the period between 1823 and 1827, when the Baptist Home Missionary Society for Scotland was eventually formed "chiefly for the Highlands and Islands". It was able to gather funds in a way that the other little bodies had been unable to do, and survived as an independent entity until 1931, when it was incorporated into the Baptist Union of Scotland. Pooling of resources also enhanced the scope and effectiveness of Baptist missionary endeavour in the Highlands. In spite of such advantages, however, the road to unity was painful, and the possibility of a united Highland mission embracing Baptists, Independents and Presbyterians was an impossible ideal. Baptists and Congregationalists were destined to be a diminishing minority in the Highlands. Nevertheless, their missionaries sowed seeds of evangelical renewal widely throughout the region, and helped to bring fruitful harvests to the larger denominations.

Native Gaelic missionaries

If missionary bodies found it hard to cooperate with one another, there was at least one thing on which they all agreed — the use of native Gaelic missionaries. In the Highlands, Baptists (of all persuasions) and Congregationalists employed missionaries who were Gaelic-speaking laymen. In fact, this wave of missionary activity is remarkable for its use of native-born preachers from the outset. Although the origins of this movement lay outside the Highlands, it soon became indigenous and capitalized on "internal recruitment" within three key localities where Baptist and Congregational churches were planted — Highland Perthshire, from Loch Tay to Rannoch; Strathspey; and latterly the Inner Hebrides. From 1797 to about 1850, over eighty Gaelic-speaking missionaries were active in the Highlands, the majority Baptists and Congregationalists.

Another characteristic of the personnel used in this period was its flexibility. The post-1780 Highland missionary movement was conscious that the SSPCK was unable to respond to all the opportunities in the Highlands largely because of a lack of workers. SSPCK catechists and teachers operated within parishes. The new movement, linked strongly with dissenters who did not subscribe to the parish system, developed the concept of the lay missionary as a multi-purpose individual, unrestricted by parish boundaries. Congregational and Baptist lay missionaries went on long preaching tours, travelling throughout the Highlands and Islands on foot and by boat, reaching Skye, the Uists and Lewis. They established churches, and some were later ordained as pastors. They could also act as schoolmasters. Such flexibility helped to overcome some of the problems caused by the shortage of personnel, and it was effective in communicating the gospel in out-of-the-way parts of the Highlands.

The Gaelic school movement

Most Highland 19th-century missionaries and ministers preached and taught through the medium of Gaelic. As the main aim of the movement was salvation rather than civilization, the mother tongue was quick and effective in communicating with the people. This, of course, was a strategy quite different from that of the SSPCK in the earlier 18th century. Nevertheless, the SSPCK had contributed to the change by undertaking the translation of the Bible into Gaelic (1767-1801). The new missionary movement built on this achievement by developing Gaelic school societies, which taught Highlanders of all ages to read the Gaelic Bible. The first of these societies was the Edinburgh Society for the Support of Gaelic Schools, founded in November 1810 largely through the initiative of Christopher Anderson, who acted for many years as a secretary of the society.

The Gaelic schools were perhaps the most powerful of all missionary forces within the Highlands. They were "circulating" schools, moving round the parishes, and were tremendously effective in spreading Gaelic (and later English) literacy. The reading of the Bible generally throughout the Highlands encouraged the growth of a deep spirituality which frequently broke out in the form of revivals and awakenings, such as the major revival which began in Skye in 1841-42 through the influence of a Gaelic schoolteacher and spread to the surrounding islands.

But perhaps the most significant feature of the Gaelic schools was their interdenominational nature. They involved the cooperation of all the Protestant denominations and bodies active in the Highlands, and the established church was glad to encourage them, provided that the schoolmasters did not undermine the authority of the minister by preaching in the parish (which sometimes happened). Ironically, however, the most lasting result of the Gaelic schools, and indeed of the wider missionary movement to which they belonged, was the creation of the massive Highland wing of the Free Church of Scotland which seceded from the established Church of Scotland, ostensibly on the issue of patronage (the right of landlords to appoint ministers) in the disruption of 1843.

The Presbyterian churches after 1750

Although conducted primarily by evangelical agencies beyond the Presbyterian church, the vigorous process of evangelization which took place in the Scottish Highlands after 1750 was supported by existing evangelical ministers of the established church. Gradually the established church itself became more closely identified with evangelicalism. Evangelical ministers moved into key areas, such as the island of Lewis, which is said to have received its first evangelical minister, Alexander MacLeod, in 1824. Mac-Leod was introduced to Lewis through the patronage of the island's proprietress, Mrs Stewart MacKenzie of Seaforth. In Skye the strength of missionary endeavour was such that it helped to change the character of the local wing of the established church. Such processes operated elsewhere, bringing new life and new tensions to existing ecclesiastical arrangements.

The mobility and flexibility inherent in the missionary movement imparted a new dynamism to areas in which Presbyterianism was already present. Certain ministers of the established church in the north acquired a reputation for itinerant preaching, the most notable being John MacDonald of Ferintosh (1779-1849) who travelled throughout the Highlands and was at the centre of many awakenings in places as far apart as Breadalbane (Perthshire) and St Kilda. More than any other minister, MacDonald helped to spread the new evangelicalism with its stress on personal experience of saving faith.

The penetration of the missionary movement and its associated deeply personal form of evangelism not only sowed the seeds of the disruption in the Highlands; it also heightened a fundamental tension within Highland Reformed spirituality as a whole — the tension between doctrine and experience. The solemn spirituality of the Puritan kind, introduced to the northern Highlands in the 17th century and disseminated more generally by catechizing, was now interacting vigorously with a more experiential form of faith which expressed itself regularly in effervescent revivals or awakenings. Although localized revival movements occurred in the Highlands from the late 17th century, especially at times of persecution and political stress, and sometimes released deep emotions, the post-1800 revivals were often accompanied by particularly powerful physical and emotional manifestations.

Evangelicalism promoted reformation of existing structures as well as revitalization of cold faith. In parishes previously held by Moderate ministers, their evangelical successors often slashed communion rolls and some laid down strict terms for the baptism of infants. Communion services, regularly conducted in the open air and attracting vast numbers of people from neighbouring parishes, were focal points for secular pleasure and revelry (including games and feats of physical strength) during the Moderate era, but under evangelical leadership they became religious conventions, times of intense spiritual interest, which were frequently associated with revivals.

The particularly sacred significance attached to the Lord's supper in Highland evangelicalism since 1800 is largely responsible for the small size of communicant membership in most of the Presbyterian churches in the region. Their membership is supplemented by a large number of "adherents" who are regular attenders at church, but who do not consider themselves worthy of participating in communion. The evangelical impulse in the Highlands set very high standards for the soul and for the body.

From savages to Sabbatarians

The transforming influence of evangelicalism contributed to a significant change of image for the Scottish Highlands. Instead of being seen as the land of barbarians, it was perceived as the home of spiritual purity — the land of religious revival rather than the land of political rebellion. Highlanders were more inclined to rebel against the desecration of the Lord's day than to rail against the current monarch. Their spiritual leaders, however, took it upon themselves to remind the monarch of the need to keep the sabbath. Highlanders were seen to be loyal to God and to the crown.

This transformation tended to reduce the perception of the Highlands as an area of mission. In addition, the progressive loss of Gaelic in the mainland Highlands meant that cultural differentiation, which had been an important stimulus to mission, was no longer so persuasive in encouraging missionary enterprise. Through religious experience and the arrival of better roads and other communications, the Highlands were, by 1900, well on their way to becoming an integral part of greater Britain.

The Highlands, in short, ceased to be a distinct mission field; Gaelic was now frequently perceived as the marker of spiritual devotion, rather than the language of infidelity. The challenge to promote the faith, especially in its Gaelic form, came to rest increasingly with individual churches in the localities where the language was spoken. Support was given by denominational funds, at appropriate levels, to provide "missionaries" (in effect, ministerial assistants) in addition to ministers, thus continuing the formal concept of mission.

Nevertheless, it is evident that the churches within the various denominations are losing their missionary impetus, and have gone into "pastoral mode" rather than "evangelistic mode". Maintenance, rather than mission, is perhaps the keynote of the closing years of the 20th century.

Meeting modernity

The local churches have also had to work out their response to the Gaelic culture of the Highlands. The ways in which they have responded is the concern of the next section of this booklet. By and large, the majority of churches have worked within the Gaelic culture of the region, giving priority to Gaelic preaching and Gaelic modes of worship. Yet, as the 21st century approaches, all is not well. Increasingly, English has been making inroads into the Highlands, through the mass media as well as through education. As English has come to dominate, cultural conventions have changed, and the churches, once comfortably at home in the Gaelic context, are having to make major decisions with regard to the continuing use of Gaelic. If the period from 1800 to 1950 can be regarded as the heyday of the "Gaelic indigenized model" of worship, the years since 1950 have seen the emergence of what may be termed "post-indigenization", in which Gaelic ministry has had to be supplemented with English ministry, and non-Gaelic-speaking ministers have come to charges where Gaelic is still spoken. These developments too will be considered in the next part of the booklet.

4. The Churches and Gaelic Culture

Protestantism

The Gaelic language was bonded effectively to evangelical experience through its use as the primary medium in the foundational stages of the evangelization of the Highlands. The bonding was very strong and has proved lasting.

The advent of Gaelic-based evangelicalism involved gains and losses for the Gaelic people. This was because the type of Presbyterianism which came into the Highlands, in its most profoundly evangelical forms, had cultural ambivalence at its heart. On the one hand, evangelical Presbyterianism sought to create a separated community, in the world but not of the world. The true community of Christ could not therefore embrace the totality of the culture in which it operated. On the other hand, it aspired to enter the wider unconverted world, and to subject it to Christian control, by inculcating adherence to the moral law, and for this reason certain parts of the culture had to be embraced.

The penetration of evangelicalism had positive effects on Highland society. Deep religious experiences, through the revivals, gave people a new sense of self-worth which aided their physical survival. They used that renewed confidence to fight against some of the injustices perpetrated against them by landlords during the period known as the "Highland clearances" (c. 1770-1860). In the 1880s some of their leaders, notably Donald MacCallum (1849-1929), developed an early form of liberation theology in the fight for social justice in the late 19th century.

There were negative dimensions too. The eventual triumph of evangelicalism provided something of a doctrinal straitjacket, which, while encouraging the use of the secular culture as a vehicle for certain aspects of evangelicalism, set very clear limits to cultural, social and political involvement. Some writers have argued that submissiveness to God's will restricted Highlanders' capacity to resist oppression during the clearances. It is certainly evident that evangelicalism tended to inculcate obedience to higher authority, and to curtail interaction with the secular world.

We will now consider (1) the ways in which the expression of the Protestant faith in the Highlands was influenced by cultural factors, and (2) the approaches of the churches to Gaelic language and secular culture.

1. INFLUENCE OF CULTURE ON EXPRESSION OF FAITH

It is very difficult to be entirely certain about the cultural factors which most significantly affected the expression of the Christian faith in the Highlands, especially within the Protestant fold. One can safely assume that "Highland religion" derived some of its shape from the culture. The difficulty in going beyond this assumption lies in the extent to which the Christian faith has itself imparted to the culture those features which are now regarded as characteristic of so-called "Highland religion", and which may be seen as "different" from the characteristics of the faith as expressed beyond the Highlands. In the process of impartation, Christianity will have eradicated much of the original, pre-Christian form of society, and any attempt to reconstruct that society in ideological terms will contain an element of speculation.

The features of "Highland religion" which are now seen to be distinctive include a profoundly serious approach to worship, an awareness of the centrality of scripture, respect for preaching, the observance of the sabbath, and an overall awareness of the sovereignty of God. It could be said that there is little here that has not been characteristic of deep Christian spirituality in other parts of the British Isles, but what is perhaps noteworthy is that it now preserves an "older" approach to worship than that commonly found elsewhere.

The order of worship used within Highland Presbyterianism is based on that of the Reformation church, regulated by its subordinate standards, notably the Westminster Confession of Faith. Only the metrical psalms are used in Gaelic Presbyterian worship in the northern Highlands, although hymns are now used in the southern areas, notably in the

Inner Hebridean islands such as Tiree. In Baptist and Congregational churches deriving from the post-1797 wave of missionary activity, Gaelic worship was also based on the Gaelic Bible and the metrical psalter, but was non-credal, acknowledging no subordinate standard other than the constitution and doctrinal position of individual churches. It is perhaps significant that such churches lost their Gaelic identity much more quickly than the Presbyterian churches, and were much more open to "external" worship forms.

The most significant general feature of traditional Gaelic society which may have contributed to the distinctiveness of Highland religion was the people's respect for any form of supernatural experience. A pervasive sense of another level of existence beyond the physical was strong in the Highlands, and the Protestant church had an ambivalent approach to the supernatural, on the one hand suppressing its more obvious manifestations, while on the other accepting the existence of second sight (i.e. seeing future events). Even some evangelical ministers were known to have special powers of this kind.

The nature of pre-Protestant Gaelic culture, with its immense respect for heroism and physical achievement, may also have encouraged the ready acceptance of the values of an alternative heroic society, that of the Hebrews of the Old Testament. Protestantism in the Highlands has retained a marked enthusiasm for the Old Testament.

The traditional (though not exclusive) emphasis on oral transmission of information, song and story endowed Gaelic people with an enormous capacity for memorization, which was harnessed skilfully by catechists and preachers. Doctrine, when imparted thoroughly and backed up by the evidence of printed books used by authority figures such as ministers, teachers and catechists, could be stored indelibly in the memory. In a pre-literate society on the point of breaking through to literacy, fresh information derived from book learning of this kind would be given high status.

The key to the distinctiveness of "Highland religion" probably lies both in what it absorbed from Gaelic culture and in the capacity of that culture to act as the transformer and the preservative of non-Gaelic standards and conventions which were implanted in it. Cultural conservatism within the Highlands, retaining older religious practices once found in wider Scottish society, is at least part of the process in the creation of what we today regard as "distinctiveness". Highland society was, at heart, intensely conservative, with a natural tendency to admire the leaders, models and practices of an earlier age. Retrospection was endemic in Gaelic culture, and affected the perspectives of Christians as well as non-Christians. The tendency to look back to an earlier heroic age of great leaders, preserving true spirituality, is enshrined in the title of John Kennedy's book *The Days of the Fathers in Ross-shire*, published in 1861 and intended to display some of the most distinctive features of "Highland religion" as compared with "Lowland religion".

In the second half of the 19th century, when the Free Church of Scotland became embroiled in debate about the extent of its allegiance to the Westminster Confession of Faith, leading to secession by those who formed the Free Presbyterian Church in 1893, the differences, real or perceived, between Highland and Lowland religion were of some significance in creating division. Again, in 1900, when the majority of the remaining Free Church joined with the United Presbyterians to form the United Free Church, it is equally significant that the majority of ministers who maintained the Free Church (Continuing) were in Highland charges. There is thus a case for believing that cultural distinctiveness and religious conservatism went together in the Highlands.

However, it is incorrect to suppose that the Protestant church in the Highlands was, or is, nothing more than a working museum of the Scottish Reformation. Some of its distinctive flavour and ambience can be said to derive from its interaction with the culture, though here too the forces of conservatism have been active. We may now consider specific aspects of the relationship between sacred and secular in the Scottish Highlands.

2. APPROACHES TO GAELIC LANGUAGE AND SECULAR CULTURE

It has become commonplace to argue that, since the arrival of the Reformation in the Highlands, a great gulf has become entrenched between the sacred and the secular. According to one recent writer, "the church seemed determined to effect a total separation between the sacred and the secular". Although such a separation may have been, and may continue to be, the overall goal of the more severe evangelical bodies, the church as a whole has interacted, both positively and negatively, with Gaelic culture at many levels. Religion can never be divorced from the culture in which it takes root.

Language

Language has formed the main bridge between the churches, their missionary bodies and Gaelic culture. It is evident that the attitudes and approaches of these agencies to Gaelic (and to some extent to the culture) have changed with time, and it is dangerous to generalize. The following attitudes to the language have been apparent across the centuries.

a) *Gaelic as the cause of barbarism:* Bodies with a strong pedagogic interest in the civilizing of the Highlands tended to view Gaelic as the cause of the barbarism perceived within the region. As we have seen, the Society in Scotland for the Propagation of Christian Knowledge (SSPCK) pursued a vigorous anti-Gaelic policy until the mid-18th century, before changing its strategy to a more accommodating use of the mother tongue. On the whole, the Protestant churches have taken a much more positive view of the use of Gaelic than that prevailing in the schools. Acknowledging its importance as a medium of worship, the mainline denominations have attempted to recruit Gaelic-speaking ministers for service in the Highlands, though adequate academic instruction in Gaelic was not provided until the end of the 19th century, and even then it was not properly wedded to a curriculum in divinity (see chap. 5).

b) *Gaelic as the vehicle of Christian instruction:* The Protestant churches in the Highlands, together with the majority of post-1790 missionary bodies, strongly embraced Gaelic as a medium of spiritual communication and instruction. The success of the Gaelic school movement in particular forged a strong bond between evangelical spirituality and language, and this was reinforced by the churches. The Free Church and its ministers set great value by the use of the Gaelic language. Thomas McLauchlan, a Free Church minister in Edinburgh and a distinguished Gaelic academic scholar, went so far as to claim in 1875 that

> for a Highland minister, Gaelic is more important than Greek. I know it is so at least to me, and that... by means of the Gaelic I am able to preach to them the full gospel of the grace of God.

Generally, the use of the language as the vehicle of gospel preaching has been fairly well maintained within the churches until the present century, but cracks are beginning to appear in the consensus (see point e below). The need for the churches to use Gaelic has, however, declined greatly; the number of Gaelic-essential charges (i.e. charges which stipulate that the minister must have Gaelic) within the Church of Scotland has fallen drastically since 1945. The most obvious change is that Gaelic-essential charges have disappeared completely from the mainland (with the exception of Gaelic charges in Glasgow and Edinburgh), and are now confined to the Outer Hebrides. The churches are not resisting the erosion of the language; instead, they are following the trend, and one might conclude that they do not see much future for Gaelic as the language of instruction.

c) *Gaelic as the vehicle of worship:* The shape of Gaelic religious language was set by Carswell's translation of the

Book of Common Order (1567), and the Protestant church in the Highlands became the direct heir of the literary legacy of the Gaelic medieval learned classes. Adjustments were made with time, and the vernacular language influenced the religious language, but Protestantism in the Highlands was married early to a conservative literary dialect which has been its hallmark ever since. This has imparted a very distinctive nuance to the style of worship in the Gaelic-speaking Highlands.

The conservative theology and tenor of the Highland churches have tended to check any marked shift towards a more obviously modern vernacular style of worship. Of course, the lines of linguistic demarcation have never been entirely rigid. Sermons and prayers, which would have been largely extemporary in the evangelical context, encouraged an extraordinarily rich and powerful blend of Gaelic registers, both vernacular and classical (as in the fine sermons of Ewen MacDiarmid, published in 1804), but the existence of printed texts maintained the primacy of the classical style, especially within regular worship. It was not until 1980 that the Gospel of Mark was translated afresh into a form of Gaelic significantly closer to modern speech.

The Protestant bodies in the Highlands have shown very effectively how language alone can give a particular shape to religious expression. The medieval classical inheritance is preserved to this day in the language of the Protestant churches. Historically, this has undoubtedly helped Gaelic by providing a form of the language skilfully honed and developed for use within what socio-linguists call the "higher domains".

Nevertheless, in recent years such linguistic distinctiveness has become a problem, and to maintain effectively this form of language is one of the challenges currently facing the churches in the Highlands. There are many young people today who, through the decline of regular church-going, simply do not understand the Gaelic of religious discourse, and Gaelic religious vocabulary is being lost.

As vernacular Gaelic gains more space in the media, especially on television, a sharp contrast of style and content is emerging between religious activities and their secular counterparts. There is great need to develop a modern form or forms of religious language, capable of reaching people, young and old, across a range of linguistic levels. Paradoxically, the affirmative role of the church has imparted a certain rigidity to the classically-based style of Gaelic as the most acceptable form of language in which to address the Almighty.

d) *Gaelic as the protector of doctrine:* The Gaelic cultural zone, somewhat inaccessible behind the mountains separating it from the Lowlands, allowed older doctrinal certainties and traditional perspectives to resist external erosion. The importance of the Gaelic language itself as a means to preserve religious doctrine and "distinctive" practices was acknowledged in the 19th century. According to a Free Church minister in Inverness, writing in 1858, the Gaelic language had been a "line of circumvallation that had prevented many sectaries from entering the Highlands". This tends to overlook the fact that "sectaries" could, and did, speak Gaelic. Nevertheless, the view that Gaelic was a useful antidote to liberal "poison" was prevalent in the later 19th century, though it is hardly so regarded in the present day. The 1858 quotation is significant as an indication of how attitudes to Gaelic had changed; the language which was once regarded as a primary cause of barbarism had now come to be seen as essential to the maintenance of gospel purity and, by implication, to have special powers as a medium of preservation, enjoying the favour of God himself.

e) *Gaelic as an outmoded medium:* This is a modern perception, which has become evident in the last twenty years. It has been expressed by a minority of ministers, in the more conservative evangelical bodies (notably Free Presbyterians), who are aware that the number of Gaelic-speaking candidates for their denomination is in serious decline. The Almighty, it is claimed, no longer favours the use of Gaelic, since he would have ensured the supply of Gaelic ministers if he did. The position is one of despair, to say nothing of its implication that a denominational problem can be interpreted as an indicator of the divine will for the Gaelic language.

The problem arises from the fact that, for most denominations, Gaelic-speaking ministers have indeed emerged from the communities themselves, without any formal ecclesiastical strategy which would ensure some degree of continuity, and without the prospect of training of any kind in the use of Gaelic in a specifically ecclesiastical context. This is perhaps most clearly illustrated in the case of the Baptists, whose supply of Gaelic-preaching ministers, generated primarily by revival movements, was in danger by the 1920s and had come to an end (in practical terms) by 1965. The evangelical assumption that God will provide preachers has probably restricted, if not actually prevented, the exercise of the human responsibility of purposeful planning in this critically important area.

Although only one minister has openly expressed his despair about Gaelic, there is reason to believe that, as English becomes increasingly dominant in the Gaelic communities, ministers will turn more readily to English, and that individual Free Presbyterians will not be alone in seeing Gaelic as outmoded. Linguistic fate and religious fatalism may be closely linked, especially in the context of the smaller denominations.

Tales and storytelling

The church, especially in its Protestant form, has tended to be wary of aspects of secular culture other than language. It has proved easier to harness language for religious purposes than to employ the folk-tale for similar ends. In addition, the tales of the people could be seen as containing a pagan value-system which was antithetical to Christian values. The evangelical movement thus gave little place to the cultivation of formal modes of discourse other than the sermon and the prayer and, alongside other corrosive forces within Gaelic society, caused active oral transmission of Gaelic folk-tales to become passive. The acceptance of the Gaelic scriptures as "The Truth" has militated against the emergence of "untruthful" fiction and may even have retarded the cultivation of the folk-tale.

The earliest example of this view, however, predates the evangelical movement and is found in the work of John Carswell in 1567. In his epistle to the reader at the beginning of his translation, he directed some criticism against those members of the learned classes who, for worldly gain, devoted themselves to the creation of "lying, hurtful" tales about mythological figures and the secular heroes. The first book produced by Protestantism in the Highlands thus set its face against the cultivation of secular literature rather than the development of sacred literature. This tendency is therefore much earlier than the 19th century, and indeed the rivalry between sacred truth and secular fiction is earlier than the Reformation. Nor is it peculiarly a Gaelic or Highland phenomenon; it has existed in many guises and in many places throughout the centuries.

To balance this rather negative picture, we should note that ministers of the churches were among the foremost recorders and editors of Gaelic tales in the Highlands prior to the establishment of institutions such as the School of Scottish Studies in 1951. Although it is true that Moderate (rather than evangelical) ministers were the principal collectors of the tales, it must be noted that evangelical Gaelic sermons were (and still are) often illustrated with anecdotes which present the message in readily memorable forms. Early 19th-century evangelical ministers were experts at contextualizing their messages in the form of stories which would be absorbed readily by the community. In so doing, they followed the example of traditional story-telling. The evangelical community also generated its own fund of stories and tales about its spiritual heroes — ministers, catechists and missionaries within the churches.

Secular customs

Gaelic tales would have been related at traditional *cèilidhs*, gatherings of the community in which songs were sung, stories recited, and news and information passed on. These gatherings remained a feature of most parts of the Highlands and Islands until the late 19th century. Their demise was not caused solely by the hostility of the church, as is sometimes claimed; they declined and died out, not through the intrusion of the clergy, but through progressive social change and the influence of the more subtly pervasive world of the mass media and the decay of the corporate life of the Gaelic communities.

While the church cannot take sole responsibility for the decline of the *cèilidh*-house, it did play an active role in suppressing secular customs more generally. The Protestant church in the Highlands, in its most militant mood, took a very firm stand against certain of them. These often included customs, or in its view abuses, associated with excessive consumption of alcohol: baptisms, marriages, wakes and funerals in particular were strictly controlled from the 17th century onwards, though with varying degrees of success.

However, this sort of intervention was not peculiar to the Protestant church in the Highlands, nor was it directed solely at Gaelic-based culture. Protestantism, especially in its evangelical form, aimed at moral improvement, and similar moral stricture can be found in other non-Gaelic contexts — for example, within the 17th-century Puritan disciplines of England or even New England.

It is also evident that the Protestant church was able to find a new purpose for some of the secular, communal customs of the Gaelic communities. Thus, the wake, in the home of the deceased, was transformed into a small-scale religious service held on the evening prior to burial. Again, it is possible that the *cèilidh*-house was one of the pre-existing models for fellowship meetings of the kind that became common when evangelicalism took firm root in the Highlands. The "conversion of the *cèilidh*-house" may have aided the development of cottage meetings. Though it might not care to acknowledge the debt, Protestantism in the Highlands owes much to the secular institutions of the area.

Song and music

The rejection of particular aspects of Gaelic culture — the *cèilidhs*, the dances, the song and merriment — is regarded as one of the standard signs of evangelical conversion in the Highlands. The evidence for a new enthusiasm on the part of converts, leading to rejection of certain prominent aspects of their former life-style, is clear enough.

It is also undeniable that certain individuals who experienced evangelical conversion, and who adhered to the "stricter" denominations, sometimes refused to transmit secular songs which they absorbed and enjoyed in their unregenerate days. In this way, cultural transmission has been impoverished. Nevertheless, it would be inaccurate to assume there was a total ban on secular song and music, operating within all denominations and at all times.

This latter perception is nevertheless pervasive. The best known image in this context is the destruction of musical instruments, such as the bagpipes or the fiddle. The father of John MacDonald of Ferintosh applied the axe to his son's bagpipes after the latter's mind was engaged in "higher matters", though MacDonald himself remained sympathetic to aspects of Gaelic culture, including Gaelic ballads and dancing. More prominent as a symbol of renunciation is fiddle-burning, which allegedly happened in Skye and other parts of the Highlands when the evangelical movement took effect.

However, it is clear that not all fiddles were broken or burned, and that the image has become a stereotype, exaggerated to emphasise the culturally destructive force of evangelicalism. A couple of accounts describe how fiddles were treated when their former players experienced evangelical conversion.

Donald Munro, the "father" of evangelical Presbyterianism in Skye, was a blind man who served as a catechist in the north end of Skye prior to his conversion through the preaching of the Congregational itinerant evangelist, John Farquharson, about 1806. Roderick MacCowan tells the story in his book, *The Men of Skye*:

> He did not, however, relinquish the violin though called to fill such a holy office in the church. He pursued the incongruous combination of offices — catechist and fiddler — going from township to township attempting to instruct the people in the Bible and shorter catechism, and playing his violin to as many as desired to hear... When Donald was converted, he flung the fiddle aside, and no more is heard of it. His music was now of a higher and more spiritual nature.

It is to be noted that Munro "flung the fiddle aside"; according to this version of the story, he did not break it or burn it.

The second account comes from the pen of the Congregational itinerant preacher, John Campbell, who was active in Kintyre in 1805. Campbell records in his diary the express denial of one who was popularly believed to have destroyed his fiddle:

> We preached near the spot where Mr Haldane and I landed two years before, when only about three persons came to hear; now we had a congregation of upwards of 400 — the effect of Mr Macallum's labours among them. On leaving them, about a dozen of the people walked on each side of my horse, telling what miserable creatures they were when first I visited their country. One said he then acted as fiddler at all the dancing weddings [*sic*] round about, which he immediately gave up when his eyes were opened. "The people said I had broken my fiddle to pieces, *but that was not true*" [my italics].

This suggests that fiddle-breaking by converts of revival movements was already, by the early years of the 19th century, a stereotype worthy of denial.

Despite this, the image of breaking or burning has persisted and appears to have become a standard formula for renunciation in the course of the 19th century. Broadly, the same theme can be found in other contexts. According to this paradigm, following their conversion good pipers laid aside their pipes, the song-makers fell silent, the poets burned their manuscripts of secular poetry, and the ministers added to the general gloom by stamping out the song tradition.

On the last point, however, there is evidence to the contrary. Ewen MacDiarmid (whose Gaelic sermons of 1804 show that he was thoroughly evangelical in his theology) was one of several major clerical collectors of Gaelic songs. Part of his surviving corpus has recently been published. Robert MacGregor, father of Alexander MacGregor (see below), assembled an important manuscript of Gaelic songs while missionary (from 1799) in the parish of Glenmuick, Tillich and Glengairn in eastern Aberdeenshire. The large collection of songs made by James McLagan of Amulree, Perthshire, in the mid-18th century is a national asset now housed in Glasgow University Library.

It is sometimes suggested that Gaelic songs and music were displaced by the Gaelic metrical psalter (translated between 1659 and 1694). It is certainly true that the metrical psalter came to occupy a major place in Highland worship, and that its contents are now the time-honoured "songs of Zion" associated pre-eminently with the Gaelic worship of the Presbyterian churches. Their tunes — bearing such un-Gaelic names as "Martyrdom", "Torwood", "Moravia", "Walsall", etc. — have been thoroughly Gaelicized, with appropriate Gaelic musical ornamentation such as grace-notes.

Nevertheless, the co-existence and interaction of sacred and secular, rather than the displacement of the latter by the former, is nowhere more evident than in the field of song. Hymnology is perhaps the area of greatest liberty within the Highland religious tradition; it is certainly the field in which one can observe the most fruitful interaction between sacred and secular dimensions of Gaelic musical culture. Gaelic hymns drew not on the rather restricted repertoire of Lowland Presbyterian worship, but on personal emotions. Tunes were derived from popular songs, an art form which extended throughout the Gaelic community as the principal means of emotional expression. The Gaelic hymn, embraced as a creative form by ministers and laity alike, became a major outlet for spontaneous religious feeling, though it found no place in the formal worship of the Presbyterian churches of the northern Highlands. A conspicuous harmony was thus achieved between Gaelic hymnology and secular song, especially at times of religious revival when hymns came into their own as vehicles of personal testimony, long before the days of Moody and Sankey. It may be that converts occasionally burned their fiddles, but they could not destroy the tunes which they had learned and which remained in their heads.

Creative writing

The Protestant church, through ministers and schoolmasters, began the task of providing a printed Gaelic literature, and was the only institution to do so for some three hundred years. This was motivated initially by the need to provide instruction in the faith, though this broadened later to include language and culture.

The primary output was predominantly a *translated* literature, using English books already in existence, rather than encouraging genuinely creative production. This trend began with Carswell's work but, in reality, took off in the mid-18th century with the publication of a translation of Richard Baxter's *Call to the Unconverted* (1750). By the 19th century, John Bunyan was probably the most popular writer in the Highlands, and Gaelic people would have regarded him as one of themselves. He is one of the few "early" writers to have been re-translated into Gaelic in the 20th century.

While such activity undoubtedly strengthened the role of Gaelic as a written religious language, it discouraged the growth of a lively Gaelic style; translations tended to follow their originals, though not always slavishly; and the inclination to choose models external to the culture was predisposed to retard, if not to prevent, the emergence of a genuinely Gaelic religious prose literature.

Attempts to produce an indigenous Gaelic religious prose literature, for the good of Gaelic as well as people's souls, were nevertheless made but not until the first half of the 19th century. Pride of place in this must go to the labours of Norman MacLeod (1783-1862), who produced two periodi-cals which aimed to counteract the wooden style and narrow subject-matter of the translated works. There were other significant clerical writers such as Alexander MacGregor (1808-81), whose prodigious literary labours are only now being appreciated. Both men, who belonged to the established church, tackled a wide range of topics, sacred and secular, from volcanoes and politics to second sight and popular superstition. MacGregor's writing on superstitions is, in fact, a good example of the ambivalence which ministers could show in their approach to Gaelic culture. In the 20th century these men had few successors, but one was Donald Lamont (1874-1958), whose delightful sketches and satires in the Gaelic supplement of *Life and Work* enjoyed great popularity in the first half of this century. The setting of some of Lamont's work was the Gaelic equivalent of "Barchester Towers", and he was not afraid to deride the top-heavy pomposity of certain aspects of the church to which he belonged. But he remains unique in this respect.

Despite the contribution of writers like Lamont, the tendency towards imitation has greatly impoverished the potential range of Gaelic religious literature. Such was the significance and status attached to "imported" works that indigenous writing was apparently restricted. Even the number of printed volumes of original Gaelic sermons is remarkably low. Beyond homiletic material, Gaelic has only a couple of rather poor items of church history; it has no commentaries, no theological dictionaries, and little or no original contributions to wider theological debate. Religious writing for children is in short supply, and it is probably significant that the recently published *Bìoball na Cloinne* (Children's Bible, 1992) is itself a translation.

The future presents a major challenge. The Highland churches, still embracing upper registers of Gaelic language and indebted to external models of literature, need to consider carefully how they can best meet the needs of the new era of Gaelic literacy apparent, for instance, in Gaelic-medium schooling. It is not that the churches oppose the use of Gaelic at this level, but rather that, beyond the publication of foundational works, they have continued to depend rather too much on the retentive memories of predominantly adult hearers. There is thus a disparity between their way of working and the needs of present-day, literate Gaelic society. It is a curious irony that a movement which was so singularly committed to the achievement of literacy has produced so little in the way of original Gaelic literature. The capacity to read was evidently not matched by a corresponding capacity to write.

Between church and cèilidh-house

On the evidence so far, we might conclude that, in general, Protestant evangelicalism in the Highlands stands in a relationship of tension to much of secular Gaelic culture; in terms of Richard Niebuhr's definitions, we seem to see more of "Christ against culture" (or, in Highland terms, "Christ against the *cèilidh*-house") than of "Christ the transformer of culture".

Yet we must guard against compartmentalizing sacred and secular, as if there were no interaction between the two. Throughout the centuries generations of Highlanders have lived in, and acquired a rich knowledge of, both dimensions. Degrees of devotion to the faith have varied in all communities, from the highly committed church member to the lax adherent. The cultures of the church and the *cèilidh*-house have not always been mutually exclusive, but have come together harmoniously in many individual families. The interface, and indeed the interaction, of sacred and secular in family life have produced some of the finest exponents of Gaelic tradition. Thus Donald Archie Mac-Donald, in his obituary of William Matheson (d. 1995), formerly reader in Celtic at the University of Edinburgh and an outstanding authority on Gaelic song and poetry, could state:

> Malcolm Matheson [William's father, a missionary in the United Free Church of Scotland] was an interesting man in his own right; a splendid singer of Gaelic songs in his younger days and a much sought-after precentor in psalm singing. His sons were destined to become two of the most notable Gaels of their times — Angus, two years younger than William, went on to become the first professor of Celtic at the University of Glasgow [in 1956].
>
> Singing, both religious and secular, was very much part of family life and William could sing tunes before he could talk. There was no attempt to discourage the boys from consorting with their contemporaries or going cèilidhing to the house of the crofter next door, Lachlan MacDonald, a fine story-teller. There can be little doubt that those evenings at the fireside helped to shape the interest of both Matheson boys in Gaelic oral history and literature.
>
> There was no teaching of Gaelic at the school, though the Matheson boys, in common with many of their contemporaries, learned to read Gaelic at an early age, at Sunday school and from the Bible readings that were part of the daily family worship.

Significant points of creative interaction are thus evident in what was far from being an unusual home. Many generations of Highlanders, reared on the foundational education provided by Christian homes and institutions in the Highlands, and moving effortlessly between psalmody, song and secular story, have enriched Gaelic culture. Children of missionaries and ministers are particularly significant in this regard.

While ostensibly turning its back on the "world", evangelicalism has not only made contact with that "world"; it has also produced its own sub-culture, which draws on secular models and incorporates much of the innate quality of

Gaelic society. Thus, world-eschewing Gaelic evangelicals can be nourished on oral spiritual discourse (pre-eminently the sermon), devotional literature, hymnology and music, which have been developed in response to the needs of the "godly community". The capacity of evangelicalism to transform, for its own purposes, some key dimensions of Gaelic culture is noteworthy, and has helped to make it such a powerful force within the Scottish Highlands. At the same time, evangelicalism has extended the range of Gaelic language and literature, and has made an immense contribution to the preservation of both. One can only regret that the Protestant churches generally, and evangelicalism in particular, did not seek to embrace, affirm and, where necessary, transform much more of Gaelic culture.

Roman Catholicism

Since the 17th century, Roman Catholics have been a minority within the Highlands. Gaelic-speaking Catholic communities have been preserved mainly on the north-west mainland, and in the islands of Barra, South Uist (including Benbecula) and the Small Isles. They have been served consistently by a small but intensely loyal group of Gaelic-speaking priests, the majority of whom belong to Barra and South Uist. The bishop of the diocese of Argyll and the Isles is usually a Gaelic speaker; the current bishop, Roderick Wright, was brought up in South Uist.

In terms of their adherence to Catholic doctrine, the Isles are seen as being more conservative than the wider body of the church, preserving a strong devotion to Mary which is deeply rooted in the life and work of the community, as is evident in hymns which describe the Virgin as *Muire nan Eileanan Siar* (Mary of the Western Isles). Catholic masses show significantly more awareness of the rites and rhythms of the secular community than do most Presbyterian services. A recent mass televized from Eriskay also demonstrated the capacity of Catholic services to harness the gifts and skills of children, thus helping to integrate youth with Gaelic worship in a refreshingly positive manner. Most Protestant services recorded as part of the same TV series showed, by contrast, frighteningly few youngsters in the congregations.

In Catholic communities, the attitudes of the "faithful" to secular Gaelic culture are noticeably less polarized than those of evangelicals in Protestant communities. There is a more obvious synthesis of sacred and secular dimensions, reflected in the Gaelic prayers and blessings collected by Alexander Carmichael in the Outer Hebrides in the second half of the 19th century. In the present day, priests attend *cèilidhs*, and encourage Gaelic music and song in their parishes. It was a parish priest, Colin MacInnes, who, when serving in Barra in the early 1980s, initiated the *fèis* (festival) movement which is now an established and valuable annual feature of the lives of many Gaelic communities. It provides an opportunity for young people to celebrate the positive aspects of Gaelic culture, and to receive instruction in aspects of Gaelic song and story which are now less easily transmitted by communal interaction.

The Roman Catholic communities are regarded as being more sympathetic to Gaelic culture generally. Thus, it is argued, traditional songs and stories are more likely to flourish in Roman Catholic communities, and a substantial body of material, gathered from the 1930s in South Uist and Barra, would tend to support this view. But the collection of oral traditional material was more actively pursued in the Catholic communities than in Protestant ones in the earlier part of this century, and this has tended to colour the interpretation of the evidence.

Although Roman Catholics have been more ready to affirm Gaelic culture, they have been noticeably less successful in producing religious literature in Gaelic. Nevertheless, they have led the way in using vernacular Gaelic in the religious context, as Ewen MacEachen's vibrant translation of the New Testament (1875) shows. Roman Catholic priests and laymen have also contributed to Gaelic scholarship, most obviously by producing Gaelic dictionaries and dialect studies, though the number of such studies has been very small.

5. Clerical Training and Gaelic Scholarship

One of the reasons for the general lack of creative involvement by the churches in Gaelic society may be the absence of training courses which have actively encouraged productive interaction with Gaelic language and culture. The standard of Gaelic literacy among ministers prior to 1800 was very poor, and even those who obtained university degrees in the 18th century were seldom able to write Gaelic other than "phonetically".

Training for priests, ministers and missionaries who were preparing to serve in the Highlands was certainly provided. The Roman Catholics established a seminary at Scalan, in the Braes of Glenlivet (Banffshire), in 1716, and in 1831 the Episcopal Church of Scotland set up the Gaelic Episcopal Society for training Gaelic-speaking clergy. From about 1873 to 1878, a "Highland college" was functioning at Sannox in the island of Arran, under the supervision of the Congregational minister of Sannox, John Blacklock. Both Congregational and Baptist students are said to have been trained there.

However, it is unlikely that such colleges would have placed much emphasis on Gaelic or Gaelic culture. Their primary allegiance would have been denominational or doctrinal. The training of Baptist and Congregational pastors for the Highlands was not normally academic, and this may have had some bearing on their subsequent lack of scholarly involvement. Their capacity to write Gaelic (such as it was) was normally self-acquired. They tended to be evangelical activists, devoted to evangelism rather than study, a characteristic of most evangelicals regardless of denomination. Generally, ministers appear to have acquired a writing knowledge of Gaelic from the reading of existing Gaelic texts. Those who became academic scholars usually had a university education and a natural "bent" towards Gaelic scholarship.

From 1876 the Free Church college arranged Gaelic classes in Glasgow University. Formal academic teaching of Gaelic in universities was established in Edinburgh in 1882 when Donald MacKinnon, educated first in an SSPCK school in his native Colonsay, was appointed to the first chair of Celtic in Scotland. The Free Church of Scotland took a lively interest in the creation of the Edinburgh chair, which was expressly established to provide classes in Gaelic for potential ministers (among others). The Free Church lobby proposed the erection of an alternative chair, not aligned to the establishment. With Gaelic teaching subsequently established at the universities of Glasgow and Aberdeen, the normal route for Gaelic-speaking candidates for the ministry of the main Presbyterian churches by the end of the 19th century was to take the arts course (or part of that course) of a Scottish university, prior to entering Divinity Hall.

Certain ministers who had trained in the arts prior to divinity made notable contributions to Gaelic scholarship. However, it would seem that the activities of ministerial scholars who concerned themselves with secular culture have been maintained most consistently within the broader denominations. As a rule, it appears that the sharper the evangelical focus of a denomination, the less likely it was to support Gaelic scholarship, particularly of the secular type. It is noticeable that Gaelic scholars within the Free Church before 1900 (a notable example being Thomas McLauchlan, 1815-86, the first editor of material from the 16th-century manuscript, the Book of the Dean of Lismore) were inclined to support the case for union with the United Presbyterians. After 1900 such scholarship was maintained (briefly) within the Free and United Free churches and (more consistently) the Church of Scotland, although it has declined markedly in the latter in recent years. Baptists, a strongly evangelical denomination that once needed to employ Gaelic-speaking missionaries in the Highlands and had a Gaelic-preaching ministry (in Tiree) until 1965, have contributed little of note to Gaelic scholarship. These observations apply to the contributions of ministers, and not to those of individual scholars who are, or have been, identified with these denominations as lay members.

It is also evident that ministers of more "moderate" persuasion have been more inclined than evangelicals to take an interest in folklore and its collection, whereas evangelicals have contributed most noticeably to the fields of historical and textual analysis. The reasons for the evangelicals' rather greater interest in textual analysis of various kinds are not clear but may be related to their concern with the exposition of biblical texts and the fact that texts could be analyzed without the "compromise with the world" involved in field-work. However, there was no ardent enthusiasm among evangelicals for scholarly analysis of Gaelic material; Free Church scholars like Thomas McLauchlan and Donald Maclean (1869-1943), editor of the 1913 edition of the hymns of Dugald Buchanan and the writer of major studies of Gaelic literature, were in many respects exceptional.

In recent years, Gaelic scholarship has decayed in all the main churches, and they contain few Gaelic scholars in their ministerial ranks; Thomas M. Murchison (1907-84) represented the last of the active, all-round Gaelic scholars of the Church of Scotland, though several ministers maintain a scholarly expertise in specific fields such as Highland church history to which Roderick MacLeod, Cumlodden (Lochfyneside), has made major contributions. The decay of Gaelic scholarship in the churches is related to the wider change in the perception of ministerial function. Nowadays, a minister is required to be less of a scholar and more of a community worker, combining preaching with active involvement in social welfare and the concerns of modern life. There are, however, a number of factors which directly affect Gaelic, including (1) the decline in numbers of students for the Gaelic ministry, (2) decline in students' understanding of the language, (3) more specialized courses in divinity for ministerial candidates, leaving little room for arts courses, and (4) lack of encouragement to study Gaelic or to pursue Gaelic scholarship. More specifically within evangelicalism, there is an evident suspicion of scholarly pursuits, both for the potential misuse of time and the danger of being exposed to new ideas or even to some degree of criticism by "thinkers". It is evident that the major Highland denominations are now increasingly dependent on the laity rather than ordained ministers for the execution of major literary tasks in Gaelic (e.g. the 1992 revision of the Gaelic Bible, carried out by a Baptist layman).

Potentially more serious than the loss of Gaelic scholarship within the churches is the decay of the language itself in worship and preaching. The decline in the number of Gaelic speakers for the ministry of all churches is noticeable. When such candidates appear, it is sometimes apparent that their knowledge of Gaelic is not sufficient to preach with confidence at the theological level required. Hitherto, the implantation of this was achieved within the local communities through the reading of the Gaelic Bible and by listening to Gaelic preaching. At no time since the Reformation did any of the churches or their divinity halls provide courses specifically in the style appropriate for Gaelic preaching; it was assumed that students would make their own way in these matters.

Given the precarious state of Gaelic, this assumption can no longer be maintained if the language is to have a central place in the religious life of the Highlands. The first Gaelic course provided specifically for divinity students was set up in 1994 by the Department of Celtic at the University of Aberdeen, in recognition of the need to train students in different levels of language, and to stabilize the use of Gaelic in the work of the churches. This, however, is only a small part of a much larger programme which is urgently required to restore Gaelic to the heart of Highland ministry.

6. Modern Perspectives and Interpretations

The relationship of the Protestant churches to Gaelic language and culture has been seen to be one of "interactive tension", and to have both positive and negative dimensions. Thus it is not surprising that it has generated conflicting images among those who seek to define it. The negative images tend to predominate, and to be emphasized by creative Gaelic writers who feel (with justification) that the churches have failed to support the development of modern Gaelic culture. The dominant image is that of very solemn and serious Highland ministers, or Highland elders, pronouncing their anathemas on levity of all kinds, fulminating against the sinful excesses of their wayward people and standing against secular indulgence in any shape or form. A version of this image forms the core of a modern Gaelic poem, composed by a leading Scottish poet, Ruaraidh MacThòmais, otherwise Professor Derick Thomson:

Am Bodach-ròcais
An oidhch' ud
thàinig am bodach-ròcais dhan taigh-chèilidh:
fear caol ard dubh
is aodach dubh air.
Shuidh e air an t-sèis
is thuit na cairtean as ar làmhan.
Bha fear a siud
ag innse sgeulachd air Conall Gulban
is reodh na faclan air a bhilean.
Bha boireannach 'na suidh air stòl
ag òran, 's thug e 'n toradh ás a' cheòl.
Ach cha do dh'fhàg e falamh sinn:
thug e òran nuadh dhuinn,
is sgeulachdan na h-àird an Ear,
is sprùilleach de dh'fheallsanachd Geneva,
is sguab e 'n teine á meadhon an làir,
's chuir e 'n tùrlach loisgeach nar broillichean.

The Scarecrow
That night
the scarecrow came into the cèilidh-house:
a tall, thin black-haired man

wearing black clothes.
He sat on the bench
and the cards fell from our hands.
One man
was telling a folk-tale about Conall Gulban
and the words froze on his lips.
A woman was sitting on a stool,
singing songs, and he took the goodness out of the music.
But he did not leave us empty-handed:
he gave us a new song,
and tales from the Middle East,
and fragments of the philosophy of Geneva,
and he swept the fire from the centre of the floor
and set a searing bonfire in our breasts.
                    Creachadh na Clàrsaich, Edinburgh, 1982, pp.140-41

This poem is a picture of the evangelical Calvinist minister in
Lewis, the island of MacThòmais's boyhood. Although no
date is given, it is reasonable to assume that the poet is
thinking of the early or middle years of the 19th century,
when evangelicalism emerged in power in Lewis. Mac-
Thòmais is contemptuous of the scarecrow: the image itself
suggests lack of humanity, fear and terror, self-protection
and individualism, instead of the collective solidarity of a
Gaelic community. The scarecrow displaces that solidarity,
symbolized by the fire; he kills off what is good within the
culture, and substitutes one set of stories and songs for
another ("he gave us a new song" ironically echoes Psalm 40:
"he put a new song in my mouth"). Culture is given a new
orientation; in fact, an alien culture is brought in from
Geneva and the Middle East. More ominously, the scarecrow
destroys the collective conscience of the community, and
puts the weight of responsibility on the individual conscience; the fire, once a focal point of warmth, assumes a
destructive, rather than a constructive, role.

    This picture derives from a particular local context, and
represents the type of evangelical minister who seeks to
dominate society, reshape it and purge it of its secular dross.
Intrusions of this kind have not been lacking in the Highland

churches in the course of the centuries, and have been evident most recently at times of religious revival. In the 20th century, there are at least two recorded instances of ministers in Lewis entering dance-halls to suppress godless merriment at times of revival. Nevertheless, it is misleading to imply that the decline of secular Gaelic culture can be ascribed solely to the intrusion of the clerical "Scarecrow".

MacThòmais is not alone in presenting a less than sympathetic picture of the impact of evangelicalism on Gaelic culture. It is fair to say that the picture of the Protestant church in the Highlands, and of the evangelical movement in particular, offered by other 20th-century modern poets like Sorley MacLean, Donald MacAulay and Iain Crichton Smith, is a fairly negative one; it is seen as being, on the whole, insensitive to the culture, blind to social needs and restrictive if not dictatorial in its demands. Given that the churches are curiously lacking in self-criticism, the perspectives offered by such poets are very important, and cannot be lightly dismissed.

Prose writers too can give vent to antagonistic feelings. Thus Alexander Nicolson, in his *History of Skye*, writes:

> As a result of the revivals that took place in many parts of Skye in the early years of the 19th century, two facts emerge. In the first place, the preachers of the new evangelism waged war persistently against such popular recreations as secular music, the ancient tales and the traditional barderie, with the result that much of the native culture, developed during the course of the ages, has been irretrievably lost.

Nicolson, who goes on to describe the second fact as "a decided change in the conduct of the people, so far as their attitude to temperance was concerned", illustrates this second point effectively. He does not produce evidence in clear support of his first point, but nevertheless leaves the strong impression that evangelicalism was the principal cause of the decay of secular culture in Skye. Again, Nicolson fails to provide the wider context of cultural loss. It is noticeable that those who blame the Protestant church for the loss of Gaelic culture seldom assess the simultaneous impact of social processes such as clearance, famine, emigration, out-migration, immigration and English-language media-intrusion.

Of course, modern secular Gaelic poets and historians are not the only image-makers. Evangelical composers and writers make images too, since they are greatly concerned with advancing their own cause in the Highlands. Much of modern evangelical writing, in the Highland and Gaelic context, has therefore promoted another potent image, obviously more favourable towards evangelicals. Hagiography has tended to displace historiography as the staple product of the clerical pen.

Much of this image — which has also achieved the status of an indelible stereotype — was created in the 19th century, chiefly in the second half, and 20th-century writings have been but a poor shadow of this. The archetype of such image-making is John Kennedy's volume, *The Days of the Fathers in Ross-shire*, which has already been noted as an influential work in constructing a picture of "Highland religion". Kennedy, who was anxious to champion the distinctiveness of such religion, provides a picture of the "good old days" in Ross-shire — a region filled with solemn ministers, men and the occasional woman, who are intensely spiritual beings, with their minds firmly set on heavenly things and spurning the things of earth. The work is rather romantic and uncritical, a point illustrated by the portrayal of Kennedy's own father. This is a prime example of pious evangelical biography; Kennedy is doing for the ministers of Ross-shire what hagiographers did for the saints of the middle ages. His character sketches are like the flip-side of MacThòmais's "Scarecrow". Here is his description of Angus MacIntosh of Tain (1764-1831):

> His personal appearance was remarkable. Tall and of a massive figure, a dark complexion, a face full of expression, and a bearing particularly solemn and dignified, he attracted at once the eye of a stranger, and never failed to command his

respect... There was a gloom of awe on his countenance, as if the very shadow of Sinai were darkening it, when his heart was charged with a message of terror; and the softened cast of his features, and the gleam of light in his eye, at other times, encouraged the broken-hearted to expect a message of encouragement and comfort.

Those who may not know the literary conventions of evangelical biography of this kind might think that this was the picture of a fear-inducing ogre. One man's scarecrow is another man's saint. Kennedy's saints are drawn in sharp contrast to the "worldly" ministers who were found in some Highland parishes in the 18th and 19th centuries — the much maligned Moderates of the established church, whose addiction to earthly pursuits became another stereotype which was lampooned in Gaelic — by evangelicals, of course. It is the Moderates who are generally perceived more sympathetically by academics as the promoters of Gaelic culture.

The image of renunciation, however, has become popular among some evangelicals as a means of underlining their continuing devotion, at a time when secular global culture is increasingly threatening those parts of Britain which were once protected by Gaelic and by mountains. This image is transmitted quite bluntly and directly in the present century by at least one evangelical body in the Highlands, namely the Free Presbyterian Church. In the recent history of the Free Presbyterians, *One Hundred Years of Witness*, John Mac-Leod of the Free Presbyterian church in Stornoway tells the remarkable story of how the Free Presbyterians gained a fortune and lost an opportunity to help the Gaelic language in conjunction with a secular body:

> In 1979, the church's determination to keep to the old paths and remain aloof from worldly practices and organizations was, in the Lord's mysterious providence, to bring its own reward. This came in the form of the Forsyth legacy. Initially Mr Forsyth's legal agent phoned our general treasurer with the information that his client desired to donate a substantial sum of

money to the church to help in the preservation of the Gaelic language. It was, however, to be used for that purpose in cooperation with An Comunn Gaidhealach — the body responsible for organizing mods and other worldly activities in which the church could not possibly involve itself but rather was duty bound to condemn. The offer was thus courteously declined. But instead of that being the end of the matter, as was thought, it proved to be only the beginning! Mr Forsyth, on being told that the money had been refused on a matter of principle, was so impressed by the fact that he, there and then, decided to leave the entire residue of his estate to the church. This eventually turned out to be around two and a half million pounds.

Such statements, which do not mention the ways in which the churches actually do help the Gaelic language, even indirectly, serve only to strengthen the opinions of those who would see modern Highland evangelicalism and Protestantism generally as unsupportive of Gaelic culture. In addition, they tend to read this back into the past, as if all Highland ministers were, and are, cultural Philistines. Few will pause to consider whether there is any distinction between "worldly activities" and Gaelic culture as a whole.

Lack of practical, committed action on behalf of the language itself offers further ammunition. Despite divine generosity through legacies and other provision, the Highland churches have not been in the forefront of secular or religious development of Gaelic language or culture. Although the Church of Scotland, the Free Church of Scotland and the Free Presbyterian Church have maintained "Gaelic pages" as part of their national periodicals, and have sometimes provided bursaries for Gaelic-speaking students, they have not (for example) launched a new Gaelic religious journal, nor have they established a scheme to ensure that Gaelic-speaking ministers are trained for Highland charges. These challenges are left to the initiative of willing horses and to those who have the capacity to recognize that grace and Gaelic have reinforced one another in the Highlands.

The churches, it would seem, are happy to support such initiatives, but their failure to be the originators of new Gaelic-related ventures to protect the language within their own ranks has ominous implications for the future.

It is thus apparent that, despite what we may say about the positive contributions of the churches to Gaelic culture across the years, the negative image provided by the secular poets such as Ruaraidh MacThòmais coincides closely with certain aspects of evangelical self-definition and cultural activity (or inactivity). On the one hand, the perspective is born of antipathy towards the Protestant church and especially its (allegedly) insensitive evangelical wing; on the other, the desire of certain religious bodies to emphasize their spiritual purity and their separation from the world leads to a playing down, or even a renunciation, of involvement with the cultural heritage.

7. Conclusions

Down the centuries, the Scottish Highlands and Islands have been deeply influenced by the work of missionary bodies and churches. These agencies have adopted a broadly pragmatic approach to Gaelic language and culture. They have chosen to use those aspects of the culture which have been to their advantage in the furtherance of the gospel, and they have rejected those other aspects which have been perceived as disadvantageous or inimical to spiritual development. They have also imported styles and fashions from English, as the need has arisen, and they have given these a distinctive Gaelic dress. In making choices, individual ministers and members have been to some extent able to define their own limits within the churches, and there is therefore an individualistic dimension which must be borne in mind.

An inherent ambivalence thus exists in the overall approach of the Highland churches to Gaelic culture, and the stresses and strains are apparent at many points. That is why it is possible to compose a poem such as "The Scarecrow", and why it contains within its own limits a valid perspective.

While we can provide a more positive view of the churches' attitude to Gaelic culture, we need to temper our counter-argument with reality, however unpalatable it may be. We have to accept that the main task of the churches was not, and is not, the promotion of Gaelic or Gaelic culture. The churches' major concern is the promotion of the Christian gospel but, in order to achieve their aim, they have to communicate with people within the Gaelic cultural area, and the gospel in the Highlands, as in many other parts of the world, has had to be presented in a package which was recognizable to the potential audience. The tragedy of such an approach is that it does not perceive culture to be good or wholesome in itself; it is seen primarily as a medium for a message, and is considered good only in those parts which can be transformed and used by the churches.

It could, of course, be argued that far from rejecting Gaelic culture in its totality, the Presbyterian churches (in particular) have so strongly embraced certain parts of it, notably the Gaelic language itself, that they have produced a distinctive brand of culturally conditioned Highland evangelicalism. Some have gone so far as to call this "Gaelic Calvinism", at least in its pre-1690 phase. Whatever we may say for or against such a label, it is undeniable that, in fulfilling their aims, no other public bodies in Scotland have used Gaelic so consistently in the higher domains as the Presbyterian churches. A major by-product of this has been the strengthening of the language and of some (though by no means all) dimensions of the culture.

As a consequence of such inculturation, the churches have not found it easy to make headway in the changing world of the modern, 20th-century Highlands. If they are now tending to lean away from Gaelic, it is not necessarily because they are inherently hostile to it; it may be because they are encountering language-shift and even culture-shift within their own communities, and this may be leading to problems in the maintenance of their older, Gaelic identity.

There are obvious dangers in such an approach to native culture. Evangelicalism is concerned with people's souls, and if these souls can be reached more effectively, and in greater numbers, in English than in Gaelic, why should Gaelic preaching be maintained? The question is made all the more urgent by the decreasing number of Gaelic-speaking candidates for the ministry of the various churches. The smaller denominations have already faced this issue and some, notably the Baptists, have responded by quietly allowing Gaelic preaching to become a thing of the past, "inevitably" superseded by English. It may be that the larger churches will have to face this question soon. If they do, it will be interesting to see how they will tackle it, and how they will move: to date no church has developed a "theology of language", and no church has an official policy for Gaelic.

As we approach the 21st century, the Highland churches are confronting major challenges. They need to look seriously at their commitment to Gaelic culture, but more particularly at the immense debt that they owe to the language as a major vehicle for the Christian gospel. In acknowledgment of that debt, they should hammer out a policy for the support of Gaelic, and take a more positive role in its promotion, not least in the recruitment and training of Gaelic ministers who are well tuned in to the needs of contemporary society. They cannot opt out on the pretext of their evangelical goals, nor can they with impunity invoke the Almighty's approval of their own failures. Rather, they need to acknowledge that the Gaelic-based ecclesiastical culture which has been created during the last four centuries, and which now underpins the language, is largely of their own making. It will then follow logically that they must assume some degree of responsibility for the future development of Gaelic culture, in a manner consistent with the needs of modern Gaelic society. To act otherwise will tarnish and debase the message of the gospel by demonstrating that the churches have embraced the Gaelic language — and the "usable" parts of its culture — on a purely utilitarian basis, as no more than a means to an end.

Select Bibliography

This booklet draws extensively on two earlier articles by the author: "Missions and Movements for the Evangelisation of the Scottish Highlands, 1700-1850", forthcoming, in the *International Bulletin of Missionary Research*; and "Saints and Scarecrows: The Churches and Gaelic Culture in the Highlands since 1560", in the *Scottish Bulletin of Evangelical Theology*, 14, no. 1, spring 1996, pp.3-22.

There are only a few articles (and, so far, no books) specifically devoted to the attitudes of the churches to Gaelic culture.

For the reader who wishes to progress beyond the present booklet, the best survey currently available of the Highland churches in their Gaelic context is John MacInnes, *The Evangelical Movement in the Highlands of Scotland 1688-1800*, Aberdeen, 1951. Unfortunately, this book stops at 1800, and does not cover the 19th century, when evangelicalism became a particularly potent force in the Highlands. The author was a Highland parish minister.

A very useful article by another John MacInnes, formerly senior lecturer in the School of Scottish Studies, should be noted: "Religion in Gaelic Society", *Transactions of the Gaelic Society of Inverness*, 52, 1980-82, pp.221-42. The only study of Gaelic culture in a denominational context is "Baptists and Highland Culture", *The Baptist Quarterly*, 33, 1989, pp.155-73, by Donald E. Meek. This article considers the impact of culture shift on individual congregations and on missionary strategy. Although it is concerned specifically with Baptists, it is relevant to the other denominations.

The paucity of assessments by Gaelic-speaking clergy reflects the churches' egregious failure to produce any sustained scholarly engagement with the issues of Gaelic language and culture. Apart from the work of John MacInnes (*The Evangelical Movement*, cited above), the most significant recent contributions by a Highland clergyman came from the late Thomas M. Murchison, of the Church of Scotland; see his Gaelic article "An Eaglais anns a' Ghàidhealtachd anns an Ochdamh Linn Deug" (The Church in the Highlands in the 18th Century), in *Transactions of the*

Gaelic Society of Glasgow, 5, 1958. Murchison also contributed articles to: D.S. Thomson, *The Companion to Gaelic Scotland*, Oxford, 1983, which gives space to several major dimensions of the churches' Gaelic involvement. Kenneth D. MacDonald, senior lecturer at the University of Glasgow, has similarly contributed excellent studies to the *Companion*.

Further articles reflecting Gaelic perspectives, by Kenneth D. MacDonald and Donald E. Meek, can be found in Nigel M. de S. Cameron, David F. Wright et al., eds, *The Dictionary of Scottish Church History and Theology*, Edinburgh, 1993. The dictionary contains brief biographies of many ministers and writers mentioned in this pamphlet.

Gaelic in the ecclesiastical context is treated by non-Gaelic-speaking historians in two important books: Victor E. Durkacz, *The Decline of the Celtic Languages*, Edinburgh, 1983, paperback ed. 1996; and Charles W.J. Withers, *Gaelic in Scotland 1698-1981: The Geographical History of a Language*, Edinburgh, 1984. The volume by Durkacz is particularly relevant to the subject of this booklet.

For an account of the geography of the Highlands and Islands, see A.C. O'Dell & Kenneth Walton, *The Highlands and Islands of Scotland*, London, 1962. For an overview of the culture, see Charles W.J. Withers, *Gaelic Scotland: The Transformation of a Culture Region*, London, 1988.

On request, the author can supply detailed references to works referred to in this booklet.